BUILD THE NEW INSTANT BOATS

BUILD THE NEW INSTANT BOATS

HAROLD "DYNAMITE" PAYSON

INTERNATIONAL MARINE PUBLISHING
Camden, Maine

Published by International Marine

10   9   8   7   6

Copyright © 1984 International Marine, an imprint of TAB BOOKS.
TAB BOOKS is a division of McGraw-Hill, Inc.

Library of Congress Cataloging-in-Publication Data

Payson, Harold H.
    Build the new instant boats.

    Includes index.
    1. Boat-building.   I. Title.
VM 321.P295   1984   623.8'223   84-81554
ISBN 0-87742-187-0

TAB BOOKS offers software for sale. For information and a catalog, please
contact TAB Software Department, Blue Ridge Summit, PA 17294—0850.

Questions regarding the content of this book should be addressed to:

International Marine Publishing
P.O. Box 220
Camden, ME 04843

Typeset by The Key Word, Inc., Belchertown, MA
Printed by Courier Corp., Stoughton, MA

To Amy
wife, helpmate, and friend

Contents

**PART THREE: NEW BOATS TO JOIN
THE ORIGINAL FLEET   77**

APPENDIXES:

Preface

"Yes, you can," I tell anyone who asks me the question, "Do you think I can build a boat?" Anyone with a positive attitude and a smattering of intelligence mixed with a little common sense can build one of these boats. Sure, it will take a few bucks, but not many. Phil Bolger designs the Instant Boats not only for ease of building but for economy as well; each boat is built from 2 x 4s and 4-foot by 8-foot sheets of plywood readily found at any respectable building-supplies store. One-stop shopping is all you need for most any boat in this fleet, and that ain't bad in these days of complexity.

Since the early 1970s when the original fleet of six Instant Boats was conceived, many more have been added including three "Tack and Tape" boats that are much more shapely but otherwise very definitely in the Instant Boat mold. Those boats—Gypsy, Nymph, and Diablo—are in this book, along with eight other brothers and sisters for the original Instant Boat fleet. And there will be more. If it's Bolger's, it's new, different, and it works. Depend on it.

Before we begin building, let me answer the two questions that have been asked most frequently in my 15 years of selling boat plans. The first is, "I can't get the wood or fastenings called for by the plans. Can I substitute?" Yes, you can. Instant Boats are designed to accommodate a wide range of choices in materials and building techniques. Remember your common sense and let it be your guide. The second goes like this: "I'd like to make some design changes—say, widen the stern and give her sail a different size and shape. What do you say?" Don't do it unless you're willing to accept the results for better or worse. When you plunk down your money for a set of plans, you can expect your choice of boats to perform as advertised, but any changes you make in hull or rig design will most assuredly affect your boat's performance—possibly to your liking, but possibly not. Perhaps my argument is best expressed by the Alcoholic's Prayer, which speaks of things that can be changed, the things that cannot, and the need for wisdom to know the difference.

The last appendix is an introduction to sailing a small boat, because I know from correspondence that many of you who build the Instant Boats have never been sailing before. I remember clearly my own first awkward attempts, so I'm still qualified to tell you about it.

Let's build a boat.

H.H. "Dynamite" Payson
September 1984

Acknowledgments

To Frank O'Brien, whose illustrative talents grace the cover and pages of this book.

To Bill Prosser for his part in bringing the book together.

To Jeff Julian for his photographic skills and the use of his photos.

To Editor Jonathan Eaton a special thanks for working with me eyeball to eyeball.

To my three sons, David, Neil, and Timothy, for patiently making endless runs past my camera while I tried for the best shots of the boats on their trial runs.

To all the enthusiastic readers of my books and articles who have so generously given their support and encouragement.

PART ONE

Basic Training

CHAPTER ONE

Opening The Door

Take a few sheets of plywood, cut them to shape from scaled up, carefully drawn plans, smear on a little glue, drive a couple of handfuls of small nails, stir up a mess of paint, and *presto!*—you have built an Instant Boat.

So I'm oversimplifying—but not all that much. It's a fact that these basic ingredients, put together with a dollop of common sense and a minimum of basic carpentry skills, can put you on the water in a sound and handsome craft in surprisingly short order.

The process of getting so much for so little didn't blossom overnight. It evolved from years of listening to would-be boatbuilders who bought plans but never launched even a splinter, and from years of being frustrated myself, wanting to build small boats but not knowing where to turn to find out how.

It was my good fortune to live in a fishing, and therefore a boatbuilding, community on the coast of Maine. I could peek over the shoulder of a master builder and even ask a few timid questions when I got up the courage. But watching and doing are two different things, and I was a long way from being offered a job in anyone's boatyard.

Actually, I wasn't interested in punching someone else's time clock anyway. My goal was to do my own thing in my own little shop at home. But at this stage,

the door to the world of boatbuilding seemed locked. Where could I find a key?

I decided my best bet was a reputable independent boatbuilder named Sulo Gronros. He had been building boats when I was a kid, as his father Axel had done before him, and was still hard at it then and still is today.

Sulo fired back two short answers: "Get yourself an architect's scale rule, and don't use your own head when you can use somebody else's."

These sounded more like riddles than answers. When I asked Sulo to elaborate a little on the second part of his advice, he said only: "Don't waste your time redoing what's been done before. Start with what you know already works, and go on from there."

When I checked out the scale rule, I found it a little frightening. Triangular in cross section, it had a separate scale inscribed on each of its six edges. But with a little study, I discovered how to read and measure with the rule, and that any school kid with an ounce of brains could use it to go from inches to feet and back again. This is often the way with new and challenging things: grapple with them, and they cave right in.

As for the second hint, I remembered watching my father-in-law, Archie Rackliff, build round-bottomed, strip-planked boats without benefit of either plans or a model. Obviously this by-guess-and-by-God method was a hard way to go. Archie had to make a lot of adjustments as he worked along—shifting his molds this way and that, taking a little off a mold or adding a little to it if his planking didn't lie in a fair curve.

But he built the boats he wanted for his own uses, and they worked, so I followed his example. A little luck and a lot of determination helped me flounder my way through two boats, and convinced me that there must be a better way.

Then I really took Sulo's words to heart. I made a half-model for a boat to my own liking, and with the help of the scale rule, I took off the lines I needed to build the boat. (A half-model is all you need, since both halves of a boat are identical, or are supposed to be.) Now I had measurements to go by, not guesses, and the half-model to look at as well.

The result was a dozen or so plank-on-frame boats that looked good and worked well, and a heady feeling of accomplishment. In fact, nothing I had ever done before matched the satisfaction of starting with an idea for a boat, creating a model from the idea, building the boat full-size, and then putting it to use or selling it. In those days, I was a full-time lobsterman and only a part-time boatbuilder.

Still, something was lacking. Although I'd made considerable progress beyond the hit-or-miss method, I was only doing what had been done by countless generations of boatbuilders before me. I had even done my own designing, in a way, but my ambitions didn't lie in that direction. I wanted to learn all I could about building.

Let me say right here that I count myself fortunate to have started my boatbuilding career using the seat-of-the-pants method. Lessons learned the hard way and mistakes paid for out of your own pocket stay with you and will always be there for future use when you need them. I was doing good, clean work and developing skills that have given me considerable satisfaction.

But plastic construction materials were coming up on the boatbuilding horizon, and the demand for my products began to fade. Putting my new skills aside was hard to do, but I had to face it: There was no market for wooden boats that take a month to build when fiberglass boats could be turned out in a day or two. All the manufacturer had to do was to get his hands on one good hull, then use it as a male plug or a female mold and reproduce it endlessly in the new material. Soon they were selling these modern wonders at filling stations—for a while, anyway, until the mass market was glutted.

With deep regret I gave up the building of round-bottomed custom wooden boats and went to work turn-ing out utility skiffs with flat, crossplanked bottoms. In the process I began to value the virtues of plywood.

LIGHTER...SIMPLER...CHEAPER

Let's make it clear at the start that cheaper construction doesn't have to mean "cheapie" construction.

If you build boats long enough in one locality, the chances are that your boats will be adapted to local conditions. For this reason, I tended to build hulls heavier and stronger than would generally have been necessary. This is understandable in view of the rough conditions and rough usage, not to mention neglect, that Maine coastal fishermen subject their skiffs to. So in the beginning my boats had hefty pine sides and bottoms.

Then pine boards that were wide enough became hard to find and were too expensive when you could find them. Along with other skiff builders, I began cutting the sides from plywood sheets. About the same time, we all switched to local cedar for the bottom crossplanking—it was cheaper than pine and every bit as good.

A typical result of this approach was a 12-foot skiff I built for my own use, to a design by Sulo's father Axel. I built her upside down on a jig. Her sides were plywood and her bottom cedar, but she had an oak shoe running from stem to stern and another one on each side of that, both to hold her crossplanked bottom together and to provide runners so you could pull her up on a beach. Her chine logs, stem, and framing were all oak, and she had both inside and outside gunwales, also oak. Heavy? I *guess* she was heavy. But she was still somewhat lighter than the old pine-sided model.

Now, it makes sense to design and build your boat in keeping with the use you're going to make of her. If you are going to paddle around some inland lake or pond, you can get by with very light construction. If you're going to use her in open water and land in surf on a rock-strewn beach, that's something else again.

Drag this same crossplanked bottom up and down a rocky shore for a few seasons, as I was doing with mine when I was lobstering off the north end of Little Metinic Island, and you will find that those strengthening drag strips very efficiently channel little rocks and pebbles between them, making very abrasive rivers that will wear away your bottom.

But if you use a sheet of plywood for this bottom, you can cut the drag strips down to no more than absolutely necessary for stiffness, and although the bottom will still wear, it will wear evenly.

So you see, less *can* be more. Rightly used, lighter and cheaper can even be stronger, as I was soon to discover through my first experience in dealing with marine architect Philip C. Bolger. This was the beginning of a partnership that culminated in the revolutionary concept of Instant Boats.

A BUILDER'S DESIGNER

Phil Bolger can design in any model and any size, and his creations range from little workaday scows to a submarine and a fully rigged ship. But he has always found a special fascination in producing small craft—believing, and I think rightly, that designing small presents a greater challenge than designing big. I made his professional acquaintance through a set of plans for a small plywood dory that a customer of mine had brought to my shop.

At that time, I was very leery of small dories; I had met up with too many that seemed to have been designed for small kids to drown in, or come close to it. This design was different. Even on paper, it had very clean lines and a convincing look of built-in seaworthiness, in spite of its overall length of only 15 feet 6 inches.

Bolger's plans for her were drawn to a scale of 1½ inches equals 1 foot, so I flipped my scale rule to the proper blade and wrung his drawings out, detail by detail. One big advantage of learning to use a scale rule is that with a set of plans on your bench and the rule in your hand, you can build a boat in your head. Question some dimension and your scale rule will deliver an instant decision on whether or not it is right.

My close scrutiny of those dory plans told me that here was a rarity among designers: Phil Bolger knew how to build as well as how to draw. Where I saw possible difficulties in making bits and pieces come together, he had seen them too and had made provisions to take care of them.

I was looking at the lightest construction I had ever seen—only one set of side frames and no bottom frames at all. She was as clean as a hound's tooth and used not one pound of wood more than was absolutely necessary. In fact, I wasn't sure she used enough. I was even a little shocked to see that she had no inside gunwales, and when I built my first one I put them in her, just because I always had. The first time I flipped her over to clean her out, I faced the usual problem of scraping out the sand and miscellaneous debris that collects under inside gunwales. I soon learned to trust the strength of her design and never put inside gunwales in one of those dories again. To date, I have built and sold more than 100 of them.

Later I was to learn that dories built to this design had won some lengthy races, some of them in open water offshore. I won a couple of races in them myself. By that time, I learned to put confidence in any plans that came from Phil Bolger's board.

And they came thick and fast. Boats don't mean much just lying around on paper, but these just begged to be built. I built them.

First to arrive was the Thomaston Galley, a plywood V-bottom that worked equally well under sail, power, and oars. Then came the Sea Hawk, a version of a light dory with a squared-off stern and a flat run so she could take power, and did she ever. With three people aboard and a 20 h.p. Merc on her transom, she gave me a 30-knot sleigh ride. Next in line was Kotick, a strip-planked canoe.

They all had one thing in common: they required hours of lofting, and you had to construct a jig to build them on before a piece of wood ever went into the hull itself. Without my earlier experience, I wouldn't have been able to build any one of them.

I had good reason to give this some serious thought. Some time back I had started selling boat plans to home builders, and I was finding out that anyone who sells plans can expect to have to explain them to the buyer who calls up, hammer in hand, to ask, "What do I do now?"

I was getting my fair share of such calls. I had been assuming (always a mistake) that because my customers wanted the plans badly enough to order and pay for them, they had at least some glimmering of how to go about building a boat. Few of them, I was discovering, had ever heard of lofting, and unfortunately a good many had a strong desire to build a boat, but that was about it.

Selling plans for boats that never get built goes against my grain. It is also a straight road to bankruptcy in the long run.

There had to be a solution, and my association with Phil Bolger convinced me that he could help provide it if anyone could. I was counting on his obvious compassion for the all-thumbs-and-little-skills novice. I asked him if he would design a line of boats that did not require either lofting or a jig—good, sound, handsome boats that could be built by anyone with minimal carpentry skills.

He agreed, with one proviso: that before I sold a single plan I would build a prototype for each such boat he designed, and that we would test it in the water. That suited me right down to the ground.

The result was the original fleet of six Instant Boats, ranging from the 7-foot 9-inch Elegant Punt to the 31-foot Folding Schooner. I described these boats in my first book, *Instant Boats*. Stripped of all the bugaboos that keep armchair builders nodding in their com-

Nicholas Peck launches an Instant Boat from a second-floor apartment in New York City. (Bill Ranch photo)

fortable nests, these first-generation Instant Boats turned dreams into realities for hundreds of first-time boatbuilders.

These boats have been built in many and sometimes strange places—in highrise apartments, on balconies, in motels (and first launched in swimming pools), in attics, in garages, under palm trees, and even in living rooms. And I have had correspondence from successful builders in Europe and Asia. All these satisfied customers have proved that the Instant Boat idea works.

Yet there remains the hard-core nonbuilder. Despite the fact that Phil and I have wrung these plans dry of any hitches, there is still an irreducible percentage who

are simply incapable of producing anything, mostly because of their attitude.

I have found more would-be builders than you'd think who simply cannot stand to finish anything at all—some because they don't want to test themselves and face possible failure, and still others, I'm convinced, who are deathly afraid of succeeding and feeling too good about themselves.

For the most part, though, the people who have trouble are in such a hurry (you'd think time was not only money to them, but even oxygen) that they don't really read the plans. They glance at them only long enough to decide that something is wrong and immediately phone me.

There was one fellow who began by saying that he was calling from Boston where he was an engineer in a high-tech outfit on Route 128, and that he had found an error in the forward end section of Diablo (a Tack-and-Tape craft you'll meet later). I asked him to explain it to me. As we chatted, both of us with plans in our hands, me with an architect's scale rule and him with an engineer's scale (which was clearly most of the trouble), we came to the amicable conclusion that there was no error in the plans. As usual the problem belonged to the haste-makes-waste category, easily correctable in advance with the expenditure of the one hour of planning that is always worth the two of actual work.

Only once in my years of selling these plans did I ever lose my temper, and I lost it fast and furious. This customer, a minister, wrote that I had caused him severe mental anguish, but he supposed I didn't care "now that you have my money safely in hand." He finished with a quotation from II Chronicles about the virtue of humility. I sent his money back by return mail with this comment: "Ye of little faith. If Noah built the ark, which was of considerable size, surely with God's help you should be up to a 12-footer." I went on to inform him that he could keep my plans and use them to fan the flames of hell for sinners like me if the thought pleased him.

THE BEYOND

When you have finished your Instant Boat, you may find that you have achieved your goal as far as boat-building is concerned. You wanted to build a boat, you did, and you find it answers your needs.

However, many first-time builders find they want to use their newly acquired capabilities to build another boat, or even a third. They have succeeded in opening that door, at least by a crack, which they had considered forever closed to them, and they want to open it wider. Their ambitions may go beyond the scope of Instant Boats and extend to more sophisticated techniques.

Today there are several boatbuilding schools that can teach you to satisfy those ambitions. I am thinking of one that is less than an hour's drive from my house— the Apprenticeshop in Rockport, Maine. There they teach the whole gamut of wooden boatbuilding techniques, both carvel and lapstrake, from lofting to launching, when the student's work slides out the doors of the shop into Rockport Harbor. There are others scattered around the country that turn out scores of knowledgeable, dedicated builders. You'll find them listed in boatbuilding magazines.

These did not exist when I was desperately searching for an entry into the world of boatbuilding. Yet I have no regrets. Scrambling my way into boatbuilding the hard way has made it easier for me to help open the door for beginners, because I know all too well the problems they will face. And this, I find, is the fulfillment of an ambition I never even knew I had back then.

Before we take a look at some of the practical hurdles that lie in wait for the uninitiated, I want to call special attention to one potential stumbling block: the system of indicating measurements generally used by marine designers. To avoid any confusion when you first encounter it, take time now to read Appendix I—"Feet, Inches, Eighths."

CHAPTER TWO

Ways And Means

Often, the first question a purchaser of plans asks is: "Where am I going to find the materials I need to build this craft?"

Particularly in the Midwest, my correspondents tell me, home boatbuilding is a rarity. Nearly everything that floats is preconstructed of fiberglass. Consequently there are few if any stores where one can buy a pound or two of boat nails, marine hardware such as sets of gudgeons and pintles with which to hang a rudder, or even oarlocks.

Fortunately the most basic material you'll need for these Instant Boats should be no problem anywhere. In any community that has an outlet that sells plywood, you've got it made. All you'll ever need is the ordinary exterior-grade AC that goes into building houses. The same kind of glue, suitable for marine applications, is used for all grades of plywood, from the cheapest to the most expensive, the price differential depending on the quality of the wood. AC exterior fills the bill.

Wherever you find plywood you will also find 2 x 4s of the common construction woods, and these are excellent for the Instant Boats. You can rip appropriately dimensioned stock from a 2 x 4 from which you can cut chine logs, frame molds, and gunwales. As Phil Bolger says, "as long as the demand for housing

continues, wood for the Instant Boats will be available, and at competitive prices."

No regional problems in finding wood, then, no matter where you live.

When it comes to marine hardware, fastenings, blocks, cleats, and other marine specialties, you may have to resort to mail order. Old-line stores that once took pride in catering to customer convenience by stocking one-of-a-kind items no longer bother to do so. If a store cannot sell by the gross, it's just not interested.

Fortunately for builders along the New England coast, and I suspect the same holds true in other coastal areas, there are still suppliers who cater to the home boatbuilder as they have been doing for decades. Most advertise very little if at all, so you may have to do some hunting. But it is well worth the effort when you meet a clerk who knows what it is you're looking for and hands it to you.

Many such outfits ship to mail order customers. *Small Boat Journal* and *WoodenBoat* magazine both are excellent sources for boatbuilding tips and how-to articles, and they include many display and classified ads for suppliers you probably wouldn't see elsewhere. An exhaustive list of suppliers throughout the country would be a virtual impossibility, and would be outdated by the time it was published. Here are the suppliers I turn to for my boatbuilding materials. They will ship to you anywhere in the country:

- Marine hardware and specialized tools and fastenings—

  Walter J. Simmons
  Duck Trap Woodworking
  P.O. Box 88
  Lincolnville, ME 04849

- Hardware, fastenings, and ash oars—

  Rockland Boat Company, Inc.
  23 Sea Street Place
  Rockland, ME 04841

- Fastenings and fiberglass materials—

  Spruce Head Marine, Inc.
  P.O. Box 88
  Spruce Head, ME 04859

- Paddles and spruce and ash oars—

  Shaw and Tenney
  20 Water St.
  Orono, ME 04473

- Instant Boat sails and the plans in this book—

  H.H. Payson and Company
  Pleasant Beach Road
  South Thomaston, ME 04858
  Tel. (207) 594-7587

POWER TOOLS

The more tools you have, the faster and easier your boatbuilding will go, but not many builders want to stock an expensive inventory to build just one boat— nor should they. In terms of cost efficiency, it's easy to become over-tooled.

To go to the other extreme, what is a really minimal tool inventory? I would say a hammer, a handsaw, and a combination square (usually incorrectly called a tri-square). But what can you do with these? Practically nothing, unless your goal in life is to make boxes. Add a few power tools, and you will have multiplied your capabilities many times over, until ideally, you have just enough of the right tools to match your abilities to your ambitions.

If you're thinking in minimal terms, I'd advise you to forget about building anything. Think, instead, of working with the most effective combination you can manage.

If you don't have the tools you need, you have three choices:

First, buy them.

Second, take your accurately marked wood to someone who does have them and have him make the cuts.

Third, borrow them...but friendships have been lost over borrowed tools, so this is really a last resort.

Always remember that some tools can be made to do the job of others. With that thought, I will offer a few examples from my own experience.

The first piece of power equipment I ever bought for my little 20 by 24 foot shop was a table saw. Once I had it, I couldn't get along without it...until the Skilsaw came along.

Then I discovered that I could take my Skilsaw to the work, instead of vice versa, thereby saving a great deal of time and a great deal of hollering for someone to come help support a long piece I wanted to saw. At the same time, I could do the same job as I could with the table saw.

Attach a rip guide to your Skilsaw, and you can slice strips off of 2 x 4s that can be used for chine logs and frame molds. You can cut fairly tight curves with it, if the blade is not too large and you set it shallow enough so that it barely cuts all the way through the wood. You can bevel with it, too, by setting the angle of the blade to exactly the number of degrees off the vertical required.

But for sawing short pieces and for greater accuracy, a well-designed, well-machined table saw still wins out. So my vote goes for having both. You should also have two kinds of blades for each of them—a ripsaw blade for rough cutting with the grain and a hollow-ground planer blade for smooth cutting across or with the grain.

Another recommendation of mine for your battery of power tools is the sabersaw, which is very handy for a variety of jobs but which comes into its own when cutting holes through the middle of a light bulkhead. A bandsaw can't do the job unless you either cut in from the side or break your blade so you can start from a drilled starter hole. The sabersaw doesn't need a hole; tip the blade just right, and it makes its own. Like the Skilsaw, the saber can be taken to where the work is. Its limitations are a slight loss of accuracy and its inability to make deep cuts.

This is where the bandsaw shines. Even the small 10-inch saws can handle cuts 6 inches deep, as long as you use a skip-toothed, hardened-steel blade. Don't bother with the fancy bubble-pack variety, because they are good only for very thin wood and their soft teeth dull too quickly.

If you are buying a bandsaw, choose one no smaller than 12 inches (this refers to the throat cut, or the width you can cut something measuring from the blade to the frame of the machine). I'm an authority on this subject. In order to save money I made the mistake of buying a 10-inch one, and I have been paying for it ever since with broken blades, which are getting more expensive to replace all the time. The smaller wheels the blades travel on, abetted by my forgetting to slack off blade tension when I finish sawing, have ensured a modest but steady income for the blade manufacturing industry.

The power tools I have described so far represent my idea of the power saw inventory that any effectively equipped shop should have. They offer you alternatives. You can saw out the pieces for one of these Instant Boats with a handsaw, a sabersaw, or a Skilsaw. I go for the Skilsaw every time because I have one and because it's the most sensible tool to use.

Remember my second choice for the non-tool owner: Take your work to someone who has the tool in his shop and is willing to make the cuts for you, for love or money.

Note that building these small plywood boats doesn't call for any really heavy equipment such as power thickness planers, jointers, or other massive machinery. But there are additional small tools that can make building a lot easier.

One is the power block plane for mowing down the edge-grain of plywood, which is one tough project if tackled with a hand plane. Scarfing plywood joints is a snap with it, too, for it makes easy work of cutting across the veneers of plywood neatly and accurately. Another power tool that's worth owning for its versatility is the power router, and it's not too expensive, either. A power router will save hours of knocking off corners, if you do as much work as I do, and it can handle rabbeting and many other persnickety jobs with one or another of its almost endless list of available cutters. Cheap though it is, it is hardly worth buying for just one boat. If you do get one, practice on scrap wood with it until you learn to make moderate cuts, not big bites, which are apt to produce splintering.

A small selection of power sanders is a good investment. First choice should be a belt sander, followed by the disc sander and the orbital sander. The disc sander is maneuverable and takes wood down fast.

It's very seldom now that I add a new tool to my collection, which I know is plenty large enough, but I still keep a weather eye out for new specialty tools. I have a lifetime supply of electric drills, but I couldn't resist buying just one more when I spied a variable-speed, reversible-direction drill with a ⅜-inch chuck. Using its low-speed option, I can drill holes in metal and back the drill out gracefully if it catches. I won't go into all the accessories you can get for it; I'll just recommend that if you buy this kind of drill, you acquire as many of them as you can afford.

Your main concern in selecting any tool is whether it will do the job you have in mind for it. You will probably be using it for years, so don't go for a bargain price in a 10-inch heavy-duty Skilsaw when a 6½- or 7-inch is best for your needs. After checking size, balance, and general feel, ask yourself: "Will I be able to work with this tool for hours without blisters or undue fatigue?"

I look for nice big knobs I can get a grip on and moving parts, such as rip guides for Skilsaws, that are stiff enough to prevent slippage and ensure accurate cutting. If a tool is marked with degree settings, I want to be able to see them clearly and be confident that whatever setting I pick is what I'll get.

Obviously, there are tool makers who don't really understand the builder's needs, and they pay for their ignorance in unsold products. Rockwell Tool Company puts out a fine line of well-machined tools, but they sure pulled a boo-boo a few years back when they designed a small electric block plane. When I spotted one on a local hardware store shelf, I liked its small size, which would make it handy in tight places and in following tight curves, but its handle made it the most awkward tool I had ever seen. It was only a pointy stub, wide at its base and tapering quickly to where its cord fed out of the end. I picked it up briefly and put it and its $150 price tag back on the shelf.

Fall and winter came and went, and at a summer sidewalk sale that price tag was down to $50. At that price, I could use it for a while and give it the deep six if it proved too bothersome. On opening the carton back in my shop, I discovered that the pointy stub was not a handle. The instruction sheet said that you hooked your thumb around a cowhorn protuberance and let your fingers flow around the housing. That was awkward, but worse still was the fact that your flowing fingers closed off the air intake that cooled the motor. I still contrive to use it, but I won't be sorry when I've dumped it. Tool manufacturers should make their designers work with their creations before loosing them on an innocent public.

You get what you pay for, so get the best if you can. Good power tools cut down on the need for hand-tool work, but there are places you can't reach effectively with power. For me, power comes first when speed is the priority. But often, when it is not, I find myself turning with pleasure to the old reliables. They can be a delight to use, when tool and hand and eye are working in harmony.

HAND TOOLS

Common hand tools, like the hammer and handsaw, are all too often given the casual brush-off by the inexperienced workman. In fact, they call for careful consideration.

Hammers

The dimestore versions just won't do. You need at least two to cover your Instant Boat needs—a 13-ounce one and a smaller one that weighs in at about 8 ounces. Using the heavier hammer to drive skinny little 18-gauge nails constitutes overkill, and after a while you'll find yourself automatically reaching for the right choice for each job.

Balance the hammer in your hand before you buy. What you're looking for is a hammer that will swing itself, one that will reduce fatigue considerably and make for more accurate and solid strokes. Incidentally, you'll make cleaner contact and avoid grazing and slip-page if you'll take the time to rub the striking face occasionally with coarse sandpaper.

You'll also want a few nail sets to go with your hammer. Be sure you have one with a fine tip for setting finish nails without marring the wood around them and another with a wider tip for broad, flat-headed nails. Machinist's punches that have tips that cover the entire nailhead are good to have—there's less chance of slippage and less danger of destroying the nailhead.

Saws

You'll need only one good crosscut saw, a 10-point (which means 10 teeth to the inch) with a comfortable handle. The older ones you're apt to find at yard sales are much better than the current products. If you run across an old Diston, you've struck it rich; grab it, and you will have a tool to treasure.

By all means, steer clear of stainless steel; it's too soft to hold a cutting edge.

Chisels and Planes

Now we're dealing with the edged tools designed for shaping. Chisels come in two basic types: the ones you see in fancy catalogs and the ones I use in my shop.

I'm sure you've seen the first type in four-color picture after four-color picture. There is usually a spotlessly clothed, gray-bearded craftsman tapping away at a brass-bound rosewood-handled chisel with a wooden-headed mallet, obviously at work on some fine example

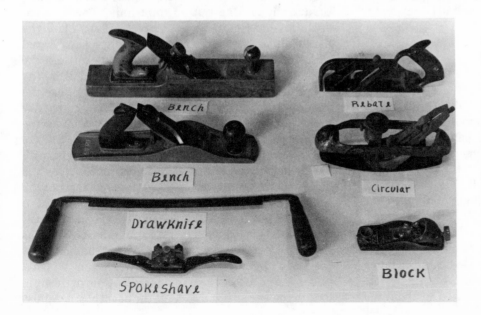

Selection of planes. The block plane is the most generally useful. Two bench planes, or jackplanes, are shown, one with a wooden stock. Both have adjustable blades and are useful for smoothing with the grain. The rabbet plane (back right) is suited for close work or for cutting grooves but is not necessary for building the Instant Boats. Neither is the circular plane (I've never used one) or the drawknife (I use one occasionally to take off excess wood fast). The spokeshave is good for cutting end grain or in confined places.

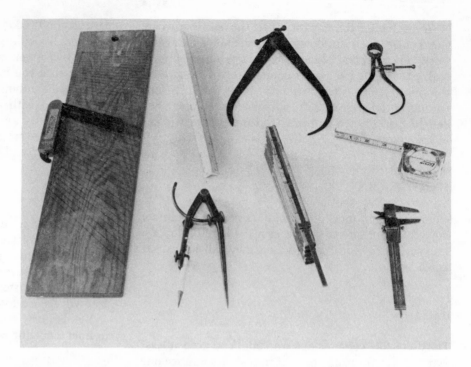

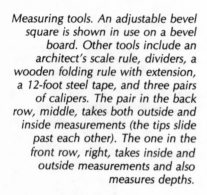

Measuring tools. An adjustable bevel square is shown in use on a bevel board. Other tools include an architect's scale rule, dividers, a wooden folding rule with extension, a 12-foot steel tape, and three pairs of calipers. The pair in the back row, middle, takes both outside and inside measurements (the tips slide past each other). The one in the front row, right, takes inside and outside measurements and also measures depths.

of the cabinetmaker's art. I like that, too; it looks very nice.

In my shop, however, you find the kind of all-steel chisels that can take a hefty whack from whatever hammer I happen to have in my hand. Their edges, though, are always carefully honed to make clean, decisive cuts.

As for planes, the small, low-angled block plane is the most useful and most used in my shop. Both Stanley and Millers Falls manufacture excellent models. A slightly larger plane is next on the list and is very handy to have around.

Measuring Tools

In addition to the indispensable architect's scale rule, you'll want a retractable 12- to 16-foot steel rule. A 6-foot jointed extension rule is indispensable for inside measurements, and you'll find many uses for a pair of calipers and a set of dividers. One of the lesser known but handiest of boatbuilding tools is the adjustable bevel square, which is used in conjunction with a bevel board for taking beveling angles off plans and transferring them to the wood.

The adjustable bevel square, which consists of a straight-edged handle with a movable blade extending from its top, can be bought. The board you will have to make, and shortly I will tell you how to go about it.

In its simplest application, here's how it's used. With your plan sheet flat on the bench, lay the bevel square right on the plan. Let's say you're looking at the profile drawing of an Instant Boat and you want to find the bevel, or edge slant, of the bottom framing piece of one of the bulkheads, so that when you nail the boat bottom to it you will have a tight joint.

Align the handle of your bevel square with the vertical line of the bulkhead, swing the movable blade so that it lies along the top of the bottom of the hull, and tighten the locking nut on the handle. The required angle is now locked in your bevel square. Place the handle flush against the edge of your bevel board, and slide the bevel square up or down until the angle of the blade matches one of the lines that are scribed on the board at angles between zero and 45 degrees. Read the value of the angle from the board. Crank your table saw to that same angle, or set it on your Skilsaw, and saw the edge of your bulkhead bottom framing piece.

One more example, this time working from the body plan amidships. You're looking for the bevel of the chine log, which runs fore and aft at the jointure of the side and bottom, so that the chine log can be beveled to match the angle of their meeting. (This applies only to the Fit-and-Fasten variety of Instant Boats, such as those in Part Three of this book.) Align the handle of the bevel square with the side of the hull in the body plan. Swing the blade to lie along the bottom of the hull, lock in the angle, and read it off the bevel board. Adjust your saw to this angle. You need to make this bevel measurement at only one point in the whole length of the hull, because the sides have a constant flare—the angle doesn't change as you move forward or aft. This means you can bevel each chine log in just one pass of the saw, with only a very little hand planing here and there to make a snug fit along the entire length of the chine.

It makes good sense to slice off these bevels before you fasten the logs to the sides, and the removal of excess wood makes it easier to bend them to the curve of the sides.

There are a couple of sticky wickets in beveling the angles where the transom meets the bottom and the sides meet the stem. But, as an old friend used to say, we won't jump off that bridge till we come to it.

Making a bevel board is very simple. Start with a rectangular piece of plywood ⅜ inch thick, 5 inches wide, and 20 inches long. Use either a protractor or the miter gauge of your saw, and lay the bevel square on it. Starting with zero degrees, lock each angle up to 45 degrees into the bevel square, and transfer the angle to the bevel board, drawing a line on the board. Start the lines about one-quarter inch apart, and begin each line at the very edge of the board. The zero-degree line will parallel the edge of the board, as the accompanying photograph shows.

Sanding Blocks

The looks of many a Douglas-fir plywood boat have been spoiled by poor sanding techniques. If you use short sanding blocks, 6 inches or so long, you'll get dips and hollows in soft spots between hard-grain areas that will jump out at the viewer, especially after the last coat of paint has been applied. Make your own sanding blocks, and make them long. A 3-inch by 21-inch sanding belt cut in half, with its ends stapled to the ends of a board, will bridge those soft spots easily. Make up a few concave ones for doing outside corners, and a couple of even longer flat ones for large areas, and you'll be equipped for any job.

As for the sandpaper itself, I go for the production kind, which is more expensive but far outlasts the cheaper varieties.

Sandpaper

"Nope, we don't have any," or "Sorry, we don't carry that size and grit." I've often heard these discouraging words at hardware stores, especially when I'm shopping for sandpaper of very coarse number 12 grit for mowing down wood in a hurry. Few places carry discs that coarse, for although customers see the need for them, computers don't. No problem finding fine-grit discs for the weekend handyman, but nothing in the production grades that boatbuilding and repair call for.

Finding alternative routes around such stumbling blocks has by now become a game for me. *Where to go?*

In this case, make a beeline for your nearest tool rental outlet. If they rent floor sanders, they'll have sandpaper to match, as coarse as number 12 and as fine

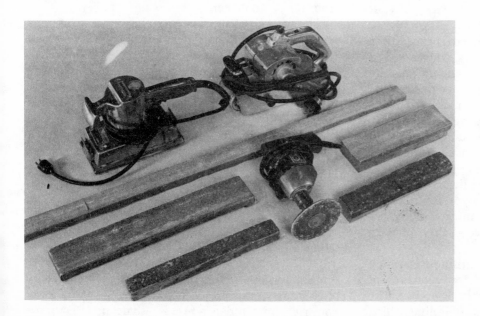

Five sanding blocks of different configurations, including one convex and one concave face for specialized jobs. Also shown are an orbital sander, a belt sander, and a drill with sanding disc.

as number 120 grit. It usually comes in 8-by-18½-inch sheets, and I can cut four 5-inch discs or three 5½- to 6-inch discs from each sheet.

You'll have plenty of opportunities to be resourceful once you get into the boatbuilding arena. I'll show you how to make up your own gudgeons and pintles, in case you wish to. Doubtless you'll find your own ingenious ways to do this and that, for boat work tends to tune up your thinking system by making it necessary for you to use it...and giving considerable satisfaction in the process.

Files

Especially when you're trying to round off corners, even the best of sandpaper tends to get ripped to shreds. Besides, if I cut a 2- or 3-inch radius on the corner of a board and attempt to sand it to a nice smooth arc, chances are I'll end up with a lumpy curve.

So I turn to files for this kind of work, and with them I can round curves to perfection, and fast. I stock and use a wide range of files and wood rasps—flat files, machinist's files, rat-tail files, and three-cornered files for sharpening saws.

Nails and Screws

Or should it be, nails *versus* screws? I'm frequently asked why I seem to favor nails so heavily. Nails are faster, they're easier to use, and they're cheaper—you get a lot more nails per pound than you do screws. Most importantly, you don't need the extra holding power of screws for these lightly constructed boats except in a few locations (such as oarlock holders, gudgeons, and cleats). Ample use of good marine glue and the pressure of sufficient clamping is the chief source of strength. For the most part, the function of the nails is to hold a joint together while the glue is setting.

Their holding power is still important, however, so you want to get the most strength you can from nails. To that end, don't drive them straight in, perpendicular to the face of the work. Cant them a little so that they grab like the claws of an eagle. It's important to stagger them all you can, too, for when you drive nails in a straight line into straight-grained wood, they act like a collective wedge.

I have an all too vivid memory of turning over a piece of work in which I had very neatly driven a long row of nails and finding it just as neatly split down its entire length. You invariably see the results of in-line nailing in wooden dories built in the traditional way, with the bottom of the garboard strake nailed directly into the bottom where there is very limited space for adequate staggering. I've yet to see an old dory that didn't have split garboards. That's partly due to the angle at which the nails have to be driven through the flared-out garboards, and it's also partly due to excessive grain run-out in the garboard itself, which is a curved shape cut from a relatively straight plank.

Silicon bronze anchor-type nails (ring nails) are my favorites. They are expensive and getting more so, but they still cost much less than screws. To be driven into hardwood, they need a prebored hole a shade smaller than the diameter of the nail shaft; for example, I use a 5⁄64-inch drill bit for a number 13 or number 14 wire nail. Ring nails are a little brittle; you can't bend their points over without breakage, but with their rings and ample, flat heads they hold very well. The sizes I commonly use range from the ¾-inch to the 1½-inch, including all the ⅛-inch intervals between.

For nailing butt straps (short overlapping pieces used to join two pieces of plywood together edge to edge or end to end and hold them firmly together) I use flathead copper nails of the thinnest wire I can get, driving them through and whacking their points over where they protrude. This overlapping joint also depends on a generous application of glue. If you can't get copper nails, screws will do.

As to screws, I use more number 10 1¼-inch bronze than any other, primarily because they fit quite a few stock marine hardware items, such as the Wilcox, Crittenden and Co. #4482 side plates matched with #4477 oarlocks, and the ½-inch gudgeons and pintles from the same maker.

The short skegs attached to ¼-inch plywood bottoms are subject to a great deal of twisting and leverage, and to secure this critical joint I use stainless steel panhead screws, in various lengths to match the taper of the skeg. As their name implies, these screws have large, round heads, flat on their undersides with rounded edges so that they resemble upside-down skillets. Compared with the panheads, ordinary screws with tapered heads make a very weak joint when they're countersunk into thin plywood. Even with the right screws a good bedding compound is a must in this type of installation.

Glues and Sealers

Probably no other item in boatbuilding is more thoroughly cussed and discussed than glue. No matter what you use, you can depend on it—someone is going to take a crack at your choice. But experienced builders pay such criticism little heed, and they are equally likely to ignore the fabulous claims of some of the highly touted super-gloops. They just go on building and glooping with the confidence they have gained through years of satisfactory use and proven performance.

For the beginning builder who faces the bewildering array of super-this and super-that, this is very uncertain ground. Which probably explains the frequency with which I am asked, "What glue do you use?"

To which I answer, with the confidence I have gained through years of satisfactory use and proven performance, "I use Weldwood dry powder glue mixed with water."

What's the matter with epoxies, resorcinols, and all the other wonder glues? Nothing except the price. And if you want to use a $40 bucket of glue when a $10 bucket will do the job, go ahead.

The next question often is, "How can I tell if I've used enough?" That's easy, too. Don't be tight with it. If, when you put the clamps to the joint, the glue oozes out, you've used enough.

My experience with sealers, on the other hand, is the story of a continuing search. In my book *Instant Boats*, I recommended Firzite—a thin, resinous sealer I had come to use for every boat I built. It was penetrating, it dried quickly, and as far as I could tell it was as good as any mix on the market for protecting wood against moisture invasion and checking.

However, as with many another good product, Firzite suddenly disappeared, and with no explanation from either its manufacturer or any of its former distributors. I was forced to find another brand.

Before I tell you what it is, let me insert a cautionary tale. I'm still smarting from the experience I had the last time I used a clear wood sealer made by a reputable paint company. Because the word "sealer" has always meant to me that it did just that—sealed out all the water that could cause delamination, grain checking, and all the other woes of exposed wood—I built six dories and walked the stuff right to them, two coats inside and out, and nested them outdoors upside down, unpainted. Ordinarily I paint as soon as the sealer is dry, but I had recently gotten smart. Whatever color you paint a boat, the customer who comes along wants something else (Murphy's Law?). So now, when an order turned up, I could say, "Sure I have a dory. What color would you like?"

But when the boat-buying season came along, so did the big surprise. All six dories had checked badly on the outside, and almost as much on the inside, which had been shielded from wind, rain, and sun. Sanding and filling all those cracks ate up hours of extra work, and I can't afford to pay myself overtime....*Plus* the extra coats of paint it took.

I no longer use these "reputable" thin wood sealers. I now use epoxy or polyester resins. Epoxy is better, but both of them produce a good hard surface that is far ahead of what you get from the other wood sealers. I use Chem-Tech T-88 epoxy for two reasons: its easy mix ratio of about one to one, and the fact that I can thin it with lacquer thinner. If you can't find Chem-Tech T-88, look for another resin with similar qualities.

I haven't used enough epoxy resin to find out about its drying characteristics when it's thinly applied, but I do know that the polyester resins, put on as a sealer in a thin coat, are still slow in drying to a sandable surface, no matter how generous you are with the catalyst.

Here's an example of a happy accident. Once, when I was desperate for time, I painted right over tacky polyester resin, not even sanding it first; I figured that if I was lucky the resin would harden up beneath the paint and I could sand them both down together to form a smooth base for the finish coats. At worst, I could scrape the whole mess off. But I didn't have to. Apparently the paint prevented air from reaching the resin and hastened its cure, much as the wax does that is added to polyester resin for just that purpose.

Paints

There are so many varieties of paint on the market today that if you don't go into the store with your mind already made up, you're in the same fix as the kid in the candy store. Epoxy paints, acrylic paints, paints for every purpose if you know which one you're buying and how to use it. Some are much better than others in their final finish and ability to withstand weather, but they also call for greater skill in application. Just recently I was admiring a professional paint job on a small plywood hull: bright red and pretty as a candied apple. But closer inspection showed sags, and I don't mean just little ones, but sheets of sags as much as 2 feet long dried as hard as cold lava.

I haven't used epoxy paints, but I've used enough epoxy glue to expect sags and runs. There's no problem wiping off a freshly glued stick, but what do you do with a paint job that looked perfect when you left it but an hour later has the skin of a prune? For that reason, among others, even though I know epoxy paints stand up better against weather and dings, I avoid them in favor of the simple oil-based formulas that require no great expertise to apply. I can control their application

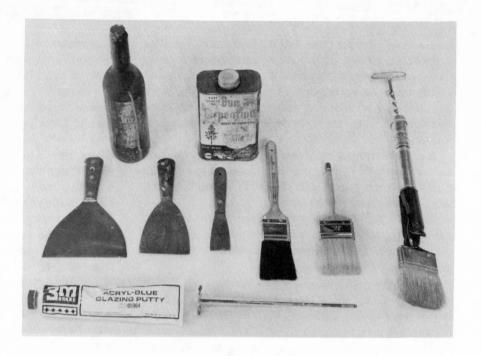

Painting and finishing equipment. Japan drier (in the bottle) to accelerate drying of oil-based paints in damp weather; turpentine for oil-based paint thinner; three putty knives of different sizes for various applications; a 1½-inch, a 2½-inch, and a 3½-inch brush; a brush spinner for cleaning; an impeller-type paint mixing attachment for an electric drill; and fast-drying 3M Glazing Putty for shallow dents. Linseed oil (not shown) eases application of paint in hot weather.

myself with reasonable expectation of good results. The fact that I can add oils or dryers to suit the temperature, and even borrow some from a neighbor in case I run out, also makes this kind of paint attractive.

Brushes

I still prefer natural bristle brushes over nylon, and for highest quality work my choice is badger hair. As for size, 1½-, 2½-, and 3-inch widths take care of all the painting I do. The 1½-inch size works well even in tight corners and on small jobs and for brushing on glue, too, though I no longer use a brush for that. For some years now, my glue brush has been a wooden tongue depressor, so I no longer throw away hardened brushes I didn't wash quickly enough.

A box of tongue depressors lasts a long time, and with a little practice you can spread glue with one as slick as slapping mustard on your hot dog. The trick to not slobbering glue all over the place is to start in the middle, say, of a 1½-inch-wide gunwale with your loaded glue stick, and work the excess out to the edges.

Every time I've watched "What-can-I-do-to-help"-type volunteers try their hands at this, they have dumped the glue toward the outside edge of the gunwale or whatever, and then immediately have gone to work catching spilloffs instead of spreading the glue. Just put a good glob right in the middle of the work and

run it out fast, as far as it will spread, with very little pressure. Then, using more pressure, go back where you started and work the glue (which by then is somewhat thinner) out toward the edges.

You might not think that spreading glue is an art worthy of describing. I didn't until I observed the slow and timid approach of these volunteer helpers; I had been taking it for granted that everyone knew.

Along with using decent paint brushes, you'll find that painting from paint pots instead of dipping and dabbing out of cans is the way to go. Metal pots that can be burned out later and reused are my choice over paper pots, but either one beats painting directly from the original cans.

I once had a kid come into my shop and offer to help me paint, so I gave him a potful and told him to go to it. We were painting together, on separate sections of the boat, and when the kid finished his, he asked what he should do with the pot. I said, "Hang it up there," pointing to the empty pots dangling from nails on one end of my bench.

That's right: A couple of days later I took down his pot and it was half full of paint. It had never occurred to me that you would have to tell anyone to pour unused paint back into the can. (Just one more example of why you can't take anything for granted.)

Care of Brushes

Ever since linseed oil and turpentine became so expensive I've looked for less costly ways to care for my brushes, and though the method I now use is far from traditional, it works even better. Gasoline cleans brushes faster, better, and far more cheaply than turpentine. I still use turps, but only for thinning paint.

I used to use a thinned-out mixture of linseed oil and turps for storing brushes between jobs, but I was never happy with it because the mix jelled up, and I always had to scrub it out of the bristles with a wire brush. Professional painters have often told me that the right mixture of turps and oil would prevent this, but whatever that right mixture is, I never found it.

The answer? Crankcase oil. Yup, believe it or not, dirty old crankcase oil does the trick. Clean your brushes with gasoline first, then plop them right in. Paint brushes love it, their bristles stay smooth and flexible indefinitely between jobs, and another swishing out with gasoline readies them for action. Stored brushes *must* be suspended clear of the bottom of the can, either from nails or hooks driven into the brush handles or from a rod inserted through holes in the handles.

Just recently I read a how-to tip from a builder who keeps his brushes in slightly canted cans (15 degrees or so from the horizontal) in some kind of bath. It looked good for both access and neatness. As I remember, he had a separate can for each brush.

Not only is crankcase oil good for preserving brushes, I find it's a great wood preservative too. I never throw it away anymore; I use it to prevent rot on any wood I'm going to put directly on the ground. Eat your heart out, Oil Barons—you *told* us to conserve it.

Paint Overkill

For some owners, painting their wooden boats every year whether they need it or not has become a ritual, maybe even a rite. There may be only a few bare spots showing, but on goes another whole coat—a new layer on top of perhaps as many as a dozen old ones. Hard, glossy coats piled one on another are the worst offenders because they don't wear off, they just accumulate and serve to entrap the moisture that later on will spell R-O-T.

I used to use gloss paint because dirt didn't cling to it as it did to flat paint, but every year I faced the usual bare spots staring at me through umpteen layers of hardened gloss. To me they looked like miniature craters, and there were plenty of them on the 26-foot lobster boat I used to haul out every winter and face painting every spring.

The futility of my fussiness came home to me one year when I had just finished sanding and painting the top of my cabin trunk. Just as I was putting on the last brushful of paint, the owner of the boat cradled next to mine started up his motor with a hearty roar that blew a winter's accumulation of condensation mixed with black soot all over my new paint job. The top of my cabin looked as though someone had taken a giant pepper shaker to it. I stuck my brush back in its paint pot and walked away vowing never again to be that fussy, at least not on my own boats.

I am not advocating sloppiness. If you feel like making your boat look like a yacht, more power to you. All I'm saying is that when it comes to protective painting, boats don't need anywhere near the cosmetic coddling we're apt to give them.

I will always paint customers' boats so they can see themselves reflected in the finish, and I will always derive real satisfaction from that kind of workmanship. But on my own boat, I paint only the scabby spots and rarely refinish the whole boat until the paint has worn thin enough to demand it.

Fillers and Adhesives

The Instant Boats concept is dedicated to the proposition that the beginning builder can turn out a completely successful craft even though he may have no specialized talents or experience. I am also committed to the idea that no materials should be specified that call for laboratory standards or methods in the use of them.

In the winter months, I build all kinds of boats with one side near the stove and the other right up against a cold wall. This would hardly be the most promising environment if I had finicky formulas to contend with. All the materials I've listed here have been tested and proved in these less than ideal conditions.

The Duratite division of Dap, Inc. makes two wood putties I particularly like. One is a white, plastic surfacing putty of fine formulation that I use to fill shallow dents and cracks. The other is a natural wood dough about the color of wet pine sawdust, which I use to fill deeper holes and apply to some woods that are going to be finished clear—that is, varnished instead of painted. Both can be thinned and restored to life with a dash of acetone if they start to harden in the can, so they have very good shelf life.

Bondo is an automotive filler that works well on most any kind of surface, be it metal, wood, or fiberglass. You mix it with a dab of catalyst squeezed from a tube, and it sets up fast—in three to five minutes depending on shop temperature. If you are just plugging nail holes, a lump about half the size of a golf ball mixed with a half-inch ribbon of catalyst is plenty to mix up at a time. Experience is the best teacher as to how much you can safely mix up and be able to use before time runs out. I confess I still throw out my share of it.

My mention of the Bondo trade name is not to be taken as an endorsement of that brand over any other of the same type. They all work well, and you can thin them out simply by adding more polyester resin of no particular brand.

Glazing putty made by 3M also works well for scratches, light dents, and any shallow areas that need to be filled. It comes in a toothpaste tube dispenser in pale blue, green, and a few other shades, but not in white. It requires no mixing, dries fast, and sands nicely.

For filling open-grained wood before varnishing, my vote goes to Interlux natural wood filler #1643 to do the job.

Bedding Compounds

If you are joining units or elements that might have to be separated for repair or replacement, Woolsey Bedding Compound #886 fills the bill. Again, I'm not making an exclusive recommendation; there are several bedding compounds that are just as good.

Epoxy putty, or epoxy mixed with your preferred filler, works finest kind for bedding, but don't expect easy separation if you have to dismantle the jointure.

There is a host of other adhesives, many of them packaged in tubes that require the use of a caulking gun. More are coming on the market all the time. You should be warned that some of them destroy the very materials they are supposed to bond.

For example, I used one of these squirt-gunned miracle goos on Styrofoam, and found to my considerable dismay that, instead of sticking the Styrofoam to the underside of a boat seat where I wanted flotation, it ate into the Styrofoam and dropped the mess into the bilges.

So I urge you to try out such mixtures on a sample before you start slathering them onto pieces of Styrofoam you want to use. Polyester resin eats Styrofoam, too. Epoxy doesn't, so I use epoxy.

CHAPTER THREE

A Closer Look At Wood

As we established in the beginning of the previous chapter, Phil Bolger has carefully tailored all Instant Boat plans, both the Fit-and-Fasten and Tack-and-Tape varieties, so that most requirements for wooden structures and panels can be met using 2 x 4s and 4-by-8-foot plywood sheets. But within the two categories, you as a prospective builder face a range of choices, some of which depend on the locality in which you live. A closer examination of alternatives can help you make more satisfactory choices.

Let's start with the 2 x 4s. Actually, because you're going to cut them into what we might call slivers to make them into building stock, you might buy 2 x 6s or even 2 x 10s. Since most of the framing calls for structural pieces of 1½ inches by ¾ inch or thereabouts, you can cut what you need directly from the planks as furnished by the lumberyards, because to the best of my knowledge they are all finish planed (or dressed) to a thickness of 1½ inches, whatever the length and width. So a 2 x 4 is actually 1½ x 3½, and so on.

I doubt if they will get any thinner, because that's as thin as you can get and still call them planks. A 2 x 4 is called that because those were the dimensions of what you could get a few decades ago. Today such a stick might be rough sawed to those dimensions, but what you buy is 1½ x 3½.

In Maine and the Maritime Provinces, 2 x 4s are cut from Eastern spruce, a fairly light but tough type of softwood that offers good holding for both nails and glue. Perhaps about 10 percent fir is thrown in, but it looks so much like spruce that I for one can't tell the difference. Out West they use Douglas fir, and I suppose there is a southern variant, too. Most of such lumber comes kiln dried, which means that a large percentage of its moisture has been cooked out of it.

I'd rather have air-dried lumber if I could get it. There's more life in it, and it lends itself better to bending for chine logs and gunwales. But a lot of kiln-dried wood makes good boatbuilding material, especially if the lumberyard lets you pick it over for the best quality and you're willing to pay a little extra in price.

I always look for the clearest and straightest grain I can find. Sometimes I have to settle for less. Sometimes I have to accept some knots, but as long as they are small, tight, and few and far between, I'll gladly take them home. Planks that are twisted in cross section over their length I leave on the pile, no matter how good their grain is, because they are miserable to saw and are likely to put a twist where it doesn't belong, say, in a bulkhead.

You'll find a few uses for lumber in boards (less than 1 inch thick) instead of in planks, though you can stick mostly with 2 x 4s as Phil specifies in his plans. My choice is still spruce or pine, both of which I can get nearby. If possible, I like to have some of it sawed live-edged, or flitch sawed, which means with the bark left on. This gives you boards that follow the natural curve of the tree. These save me work; if I'm cutting a gunwale for a boat whose sheer curve comes close to matching the natural sweep of the tree, the curved board will bend around the hull more easily than a straight piece. This goes beyond the absolute requirements of an Instant Boat; just keep it in mind, in case you eventually decide to build a craft of more complex contours. Knowing that I can expect to meet with such problems, I stock a pile of crooked boards that would make a house carpenter cringe.

Porch Flooring

Now, this may seem a little off the track of the 2 x 4 discussion, but if porch flooring is available in your locality, it can come in very handy. It is always spruce and comes planed to a thickness of 1 inch in a variety of widths and lengths. With its additional combinations of sizes, it widens your choices from which to make any part of the frames, gunwales, chine logs, and even spars that are called for. If your mast requires a 2-inch square cross section, you can cut two pieces 2 inches wide from porch flooring and glue them together in whatever length you need. If your mast is to be 1¾-inch square and 16 feet long, cut two pieces 1¾ inches wide and ⅞ inch thick from a 16-foot 2 x 6 and glue them together. Sure, it's true that two 1¾-inch pieces equal the 3½-inch width of a 2 x 4, but the bite of your saw cut is going to take out ⅛ inch, and one of your halves will be shy by that amount.

I'm talking in terms of my own way of doing things because I know what woods I can get in my area, and I plan my style of boatbuilding around their availability.

For instance, I can find no planks here any longer than 16 feet, so when I build a 20-footer I have to scarf a couple of shorter pieces for gunwales and chine logs. Not long ago I had a fellow coming up from Connecticut to build a sizable boat for himself with my help. He told me he could get planks there 20 feet long "with grain as clear as you could want." I told him to bring them, and bring them he did.

The point of this is to be adaptable and use whatever builders in your area use. I know that builders are often uncertain about what is acceptable because I get inquiries from all over. For example, I had a call from an inexperienced builder in Florida, who said "I've got a nice pile of cypress here, long clear-grained stuff....Is it OK to use it in a boat?" My answer was, "You bet."

About the only wood I stay clear of for these small boats is oak. You don't need its strength or its heft, and you certainly don't need its poor gluing qualities. I used to use a lot of it until it became scarce and more expensive, and I quit using it altogether when, with the last load I bought, I could hear the *snap, pop, bang* sounds the mill's dull planer made as it tore the grain of my carefully selected prize pieces all to hell.

If you happen to have a pile of oak with good grain and some life in it, not all twisted into dried pretzels, I'd say use it if nothing else is available. Use pine, fir, mahogany, most any wood whose condition shows reasonable promise as a material that will serve to get your boat built.

PICKING PLYWOOD

I've recommended using exterior grade plywood. Marine or exterior, it's your choice to make, but you can expect to spend three to four times as much for marine grade as for AC exterior. Both grades now use the same glue, so the laminations should hold as well for one as the other.

AC gets my vote because of its competitive price, its wide availability, and its equivalent building strength. Granted, it's not as handsome as marine grade, which has both outer surfaces sanded. AC has one good sanded outer layer, a good core, and one unsanded outer layer that occasionally shows uglies such as knotholes and dents. However, these flaws are patchable because they're right out there where you can see them and work on them.

There is a cheaper grade, called CDX, which I leave right on the rack. This is an underlayment plywood that has both outer layers unsanded and both of them badly flawed. This is the bottom of the barrel; don't consider it.

There is one variety of AC exterior I would also give the go-by, and that is ⅜-inch three-ply. It has a thick, water-absorbing inner core, and its skin tends to ripple. It isn't worth lugging home for any project I can think of. But ⅜-inch AC in four-ply is okay. At least, the sheets of it I've used have been entirely satisfactory.

There's another grade that's a very sneaky one. It's called AB; its two good sides and higher price might tempt you to lug some home. Don't. I have, and it was a very disappointing experience. I found hollows in its interior construction after the hull I built it with was in the water. They showed up in the form of big blisters on what had been a smooth surface until moisture got inside.

With AB grade, I decided that the makers put two good surfaces on the outside and throw a "dog" in the middle, whereas with AC they put the good surfaces together and leave the dog in plain view on the outside, where you deal with and correct its deficiencies. The absence of any bad voids in the centers of AC sheets bears out my conviction.

One of the most convincing examples of AC's durability is what might be called the "Ten-Year Payson Pickup Test." It began five years before I wrote the original Instant Boats book, when I tossed a 4-by-8-foot sheet of ½-inch AC into the bed of my pickup truck as a buffer against the miscellany of objects I'm in the habit of dumping there.

Without benefit of any sealer or other treatment except for onslaughts of sun, rain, and snow, plus wood piled over it by the cord, this same piece of plywood now protects the bed of another new pickup where it has begun its third five-year protection plan, with not the slightest sign of any delamination. A sheet of plain old AC that services two new pickups says a great deal for plywood, if somewhat less for the pickups.

Lauan—A Newcomer

Now there is another candidate, also about $10 a sheet in the standard size, an import from the Philippines called Lauan. I've seen it in two thicknesses, ¼ inch and ⅜ inch. The ¼-inch, which is a hair under that measurement, is faced with two outer veneers of mahogany and has a solid core between; the ⅜-inch is made up of five plies and looks as good as any plywood I've seen.

I had been skeptical in the past, having heard horror stories about its tendency to fall apart over time. Also, the unknown formulation of the glue in this import bothered me. I still don't know what they use.

But when Paul Wolter, skipper of Tom Watson's *Palawan*, told me he was going to build himself a punt out of the stuff, I pricked up my ears, calculating that after a good many voyages around the world Paul wouldn't want to risk the unfavorable publicity of drowning in Camden Harbor in a cheap skiff of his own making. I began to hear favorable reports from other users, so I decided to give it my shop-stove test.

I threw a couple of sample pieces into the bucket of water I always keep hot on the stove for wiping off glue joints. From the bucket they went out to the black-topped driveway where they got thoroughly dried out.

In a month of such treatment, none of my samples showed any signs of delamination, and one piece got so watersoaked it sank to the bottom of the bucket.

I'm now in the process of building a skiff with it, which I will abuse as long as it lasts, as final testing. In the meantime, I'd say Lauan's price, looks, and availability make it seem well worth a try.

BC Yellow Pine

Over the past two or three years I have used nearly a hundred sheets of this variant in its quarter-inch thickness. Although I have had good results, I hesitated to mention it in any of my articles because I wasn't sure it was available from any source other than the New England Grossman chain of lumber outlets.

My doubts about this were laid to rest by a letter from David W. Cornell of Wilmington, North Carolina. His views jibe with mine, so I'll quote him.

Since I moved to North Carolina, I find I have two varieties of exterior plywood to choose between: AC fir or BC yellow pine.

There are significant differences. The B side of the pine is as sound as the A side of the fir, but not as smooth. On the C side, the pine is much better: Thin cracks are the most common defect, but it has none of the knotholes of fir.

Saw cuts reveal few voids in the middle ply of pine compared with fir. Quarter-inch pine plywood runs at least ⁹⁄₃₂-inch thick, while fir is right at ¼ inch; the three plys of fir are of equal thickness, but the middle ply of pine is one-fourth the total thickness; this means that the pine is 50 percent thicker than fir. Pine plywood's greater thickness and the higher density of yellow pine make it about 50 percent heavier than fir—which explains why the Bolger *Tortoise* I built this spring was so much heavier than I expected. The pine is obviously harder than the fir when you sand or drill it. I am inclined to use the pine (costs 20 percent less) where sturdiness and durability are prime requisites and the fir when light weight is more important.

I will add only that almost every sheet of yellow pine plywood I used showed hollowed-out sanding marks, as if the sheet had stopped in the middle of the process while the sander kept on turning. Some of these valleys didn't show up until the paint job was completed; I filled the ones that were obvious before I laid on any paint.

As for the hardness of the yellow pine, I made a special countersink, a very blunt one, that I used in my electric drill before driving any nails, because there was no way I could set the nailheads later as I can in the softer fir plywood.

Despite these few flaws, I still consider quarter-inch BC yellow pine plywood to be boat quality wood. What is even stranger is that the same brand in the half-inch thickness proved to be a disaster. Its outside veneer delaminated worse than any plywood I've ever seen, despite sealing or any other treatment I gave it. The first batch I used gave me no trouble, but delaminating set in all at once with the next sheets I bought.

At first I thought it might have been a fluke—poor workmanship, perhaps operators putting the beer to them on a hot summer's day instead of keeping an eye on their machines. The factory may have wondered too because with later purchases I saw the worker's shift number stamped right on the plywood, something I had never seen before. But whether anyone was willing to take the blame for it or not, that put an end to my buying it.

Now I'll tell you why I held back from spreading the good word about the qualities of quarter-inch BC yellow pine. The answer is the "Shop Grade" plywood that I recommended as a good buy in the original Instant Boats book, noting that because of its dinged corners and a few scratches here and there, its price was substantially lower than that of its unmarred competitors.

That plug has come back to haunt me. Many readers have asked me where they can buy it, and I really can't tell them, since the pile I happened to run across hasn't been restocked. I found it at a Grossman's outlet here in New England, and when I inquired about it later, they told me that "Shop Grade" is not a special manufactured variety of plywood but is any plywood they have in stock that has been banged up and won't sell for top price. So don't waste your time looking for it.

Plywood Dutchmen

Even in premium-grade marine plywood, you'll find that the manufacturers quite often use patches, or "dutchmen" as they are commonly called, to plug knotholes and other imperfections. The fact that the BC yellow pine plywood rarely has any is one of the reasons I find it so attractive.

The trouble is not that these patches are hard to deal with, once you've learned their little tricks of ruining an otherwise perfect paint job. But sometimes there are so many of them that you miss sealing a few of them properly, and they let you know later, after your boat has been stored outside for a time or has had considerable use in the water.

I've done my share of overlooking a percentage of these dutchmen and discovering them only when they lift their edges and break through the paint, at which point they stick out like sore thumbs.

After 25 years of procrastination I finally got around to investigating the source of this problem. I sawed one of the patched places in cross-section, chiseled out the dutchman, and found what I had long suspected but had never taken the time to confirm.

There is no glue between the top edge of these patches and the perimeter of the hollow in which they sit. Moisture has what amounts to an engraved invitation to seep in and swell the joint line to a sharp ridge that effortlessly lifts the paint, even though the patch itself and the surface of the area around it lie perfectly flat. Years of looking at those patches and seeing the starved, shrunken line that appears around their edges despite several applications of sealers should have told me that. I guess I just didn't want to believe that plywood companies would use such an ineffective patching system.

Now, when I build a plywood boat, I go around the hull a few times making sure I've marked a big X on every one of those patches and have given them two or three generous doses of sealant. But that alone is not enough. You will still see where the epoxy or whatever you've used has sunk into the edge grain of both patch and plywood, leaving a depression that will have to be filled later. A piece of fiberglass cloth placed over the patch will hide it forever, and if you slather it with resin and cover the area with a piece of waxed paper smoothed down with a wide putty knife, you will have a nice permanent job.

Why waxed paper? Well, if you just stick a piece of cloth over a dutchman, the edge of the cloth will lift slightly and form a new ridge of its own that will demand sanding later. Also, the whole surface of the patched area will be quite rough if it's left to cure on its own. Flat areas on the horizontal aren't much of a problem, but patches on the side of your boat will have a tendency to sag and the resin will drain from the cloth. Be sure your putty knife is broad enough to span the whole area when you're smoothing out the waxed paper. Done correctly, this will block out the air and allow you to taper the resin out to the edges of the patch to eliminate all ridges. Leave the paper on until the resin sets up, and when you remove it you'll have a patch job that looks as though you had spent hours sanding it with the finest of grits.

Voids and Knotholes

When your saw cuts reveal voids in the plywood's core edge, fill them with slivers or sticks. Cut the slivers to

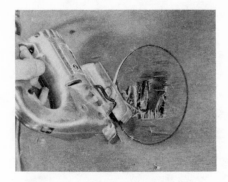

Repairing a plywood hull. Cut the damaged area out (A), taper-grind outside and inside edges of the hole (B), back the hole with waxed paper supported with cardboard taped in place, apply resin and thickener (C), and cover with waxed paper and smooth (D). When the resin hardens the waxed paper will lift off easily, leaving a mirror-smooth finish.

various widths as needed to fill these gaps, dip them in glue, and drive them in.

Any of the fillers I've mentioned does a good job of filling knotholes. When I run into a sheet that has a lot of these blemishes, I find it's much easier to fill them right away with the sheet horizontal on a couple of sawhorses than it is to fill them after the plywood is installed as a vertical bulkhead or a section of the side of your hull. By all means, top off your filler with waxed paper, and if you're working outdoors, cover it with a piece of cardboard secured with masking tape to keep the wind from peeling the paper away.

REPAIRING PLYWOOD HULLS

If you have the bad luck to return to a boat you've left on the ramp for a few minutes and find that someone else's trailer has holed it while you were replenishing your beer supply, don't panic. Just fix it.

Most bangs and dents only push in a section of the hull's side, whether it is fiberglass or plywood, and often you can reach in and push the indented area out flush, or nearly so. If you don't have working space inside the hull behind the damaged area, then you're

probably not concerned about its appearance on the inside because it can't be seen anyway.

To repair this kind of damage, grind around the edge of the affected area, leaving the indented portion to serve as a backing. Make a patching mixture of resin, either epoxy or polyester, and practically any kind of thickener—fillers, microballoons, Cab-O-Sil, Fillite powder, or even just plain sawdust. Add some strands of fiberglass cloth chopped into pieces about one-quarter inch long or some strands of "tiger hair," which consists of cat-hair–like threads unraveled from glass matting. Either one of these or a combination of both will go far toward making one tough patch; their function is to reinforce the resin, much as steel rod reinforces concrete. Fill the hole a little more than full, trowel it out as smooth as you can, press waxed paper over it, and smooth it with a putty knife or squeegee.

You can make a fully Peeping Tom–proof patch, however, if you can work on it from both sides. If such is the case, cut the damaged area right out neat and clean, and taper-grind around the outside edge of the opening, starting about 1½ inches back from the edge, until it's about half the thickness of the hull. Next, taper-grind the inside edge of this aperture to produce the effect of a circular knife edge facing inward all around the hole. Mix up a batch of your patching concoction and fill from both sides, covering the patch with waxed paper and protective cardboard inside and out. With the hole ground, filled, and sealed this way, the sharply tapered edge will hold the filler patch locked in till kingdom come, and this should work on holes up to a foot across.

Sometimes, though, the boat owner needs a quick-and-dirty method, and here it is. Saw out the damaged area to whatever shape is necessary in order to reach sound wood. Place a piece of wood the same thickness as the hull over the hole and trace its shape from the cutout. Saw out this filler piece and stick it back in the hole. Then, from inside the boat, place a piece of plywood large enough to cover the hole with a generous margin all around, and nail and glue it in place. This is what you fasten your jigsaw puzzle insert to, working from outside, using glue and nails and putting plenty of glue on the edges where they are snug up against the sound skin of your boat.

Keep the flush side of your repair job on the outside, where it will meet the public. If you want to be a little less quick and dirty about it, cover the outside with a layer of fiberglass.

Each repair job is different and therefore leans heavily on the common sense and adaptability of the repairer. It's a good idea to see to it that, in the case of your own boat, that person is *you*. This can spare you the annoyance of hearing your friendly yardhand say, "I might be able to get to it in a week or so," when your plans call for going sailing today.

THE CUPPING PROBLEM

The grained boards and planks you find in the lumberyard are often less than perfectly true. The causes are various: grain tension, moisture content, the way the lumber has been stacked, and the way it was sawed from the original log. In regard to the sawing, much depends on which of two basic methods was used: *plain sawing,* slicing lengthwise along the log to make live-edged lumber (with the bark on), or *quarter sawing,* which can produce four different sets of qualities and grain patterns resulting from variations in how the cuts are made in each quarter. I've included a discussion of this topic in Appendix II.

Blame for the crooks, twists, and kinks in lumber pulled from the pile rests at the grass roots level, you might say, starting with the foundation of the pile and including a careless stacking job, which distributes the

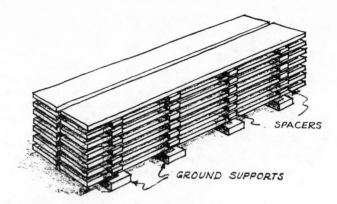

Properly stacked lumber. Ground supports and spacers are vertically aligned.

weight of the boards unevenly. The remedy is to pick your purchases carefully and avoid the worst examples.

Cupped wood is another matter, and it afflicts both laminated and grained wood. It's caused not by stacking but by grain and moisture content. Furthermore, you can do something about it with free help from Mother Nature.

Cupping is characterized by a concave curve across one side of a stick or panel, with the center lower than the edges, and a convex curve across the other side to match.

Whether it's a board or a sheet of plywood, just throw the cupped piece on your lawn on a sunny day with the concave side toward the ground. Moisture from the earth will swell the cupped side while the heat of the sun shrinks the convex bulge, and the two forces working together will do the job while you wait. Depending on the dampness in the ground and the heat of the sun, 10 or 15 minutes may be all it takes to make your wood as flat as a pancake. Leave it too long and it will cup the other way, so keep your eye on the process.

In the winter, a sponge bath on the concave side and heat from my shop stove on the convex side will do the trick, too, but never, it seems, quite as quickly or as well as Mother Nature does. Don't ask me why.

My discovery of the natural method of decupping wood wasn't born in any laboratory. In the course of years of poking around lumber mill yards, I had noticed that any board left lying on the ground soon had its edges curled up toward the sun while its belly was firmly foxholed in the dirt. I thought perhaps it had to do with somebody's Law—maybe one of Newton's—that for every action there is an equal and opposite reaction. So I gave it a whirl.

Now this might be stretching the application of my theory a little too far, but I had an interesting

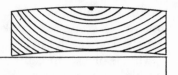

The right way (left) and the wrong way of mating a cupped board or plank to another piece. Unless it's sawed from the tree with cuts perpendicular to the annual rings, a board is liable to cup, the direction of the cup opposing the run of the annual rings. This cup can be removed temporarily as described in the accompanying text, but it will reappear eventually, though to a lesser degree if it is fastened while straight. Fastening the board or plank with the concave face toward the joint ensures two lines of contact and avoids a wobbly fit.

experience testing it on sheep instead of lumber. When I was living on and lobstering out of Metinic Island back in the late Forties, the island had a population of about a hundred sheep, whose function was to keep the undergrowth down, and because of near starvation in their untended state during the winter months, some were not always in the best of health.

One day, on one of my beachcombing walks, I came across a sheep lying on its side, and a few days later I found it was still in the same place and still on the same side. Once sheep are down they give up easily; they just collapse and die. So, thinking it was worth a try, I turned the sheep over on its other side, and so help me in another couple of days he was up and back in the flock.

FIBERGLASSING PLYWOOD

I believe that the happiest marriage of any materials I know is that of fiberglass to plywood. The firmness with which they cling is a marriage made in heaven. I'm not certain why this is true, but I suspect it's because all the oils are cooked out of plywood in the laminating process. With other woods such as grained pine, spruce, or oak, this marriage all too often ends in divorce.

You do not have to be an expert to do a good job of fiberglassing plywood. There are plenty of manuals that deal with every detail of applying fiberglass. I'll content myself with passing along the tips that have worked for me.

• Don't apply fiberglass in direct sunlight, because it hastens the drying time, thus cutting short the time you'll have to devote to making a smooth, professional-looking application.

• Always measure the catalyst and resin each time, and don't play guessing games. In general, a teaspoon of catalyst to a pint of polyester resin in a working tem-

perature of 60 to 70 degrees works fine. For hotter, drier weather use a bit less catalyst, for colder weather, a bit more.

Stick with the same size mixing containers, so you will know the amount you are mixing each time. After a while, you'll be able to judge just how much to mix to complete each particular job.

School lunch provides my containers. I stand, or my wife, Amy, stands, in a prominent position while the stream of kids passes by, pitching empty half-pint milk cartons into our waiting sack. One trip to the school means a few months' supply of containers (thoroughly rinsed) for most every mixing process in the shop. Just before the end of school in the spring we really load up to make sure we'll be fully instrumented until fall. I find that a half-pint carton, when fully open, will hold a pint of resin.

• Follow a logical procedure, depending on the area to be covered and the type of surface.

Always clean any area to free it from dust and dirt. Use acetone to remove oily spots such as spills of machine or paint oils.

In glassing large areas, give the wood a coat of resin and let it sink in and "kick off" (nearly harden) before you apply the cloth. This is especially important when you're glassing the whole side of your boat or its entire bottom, so you won't find yourself halfway through the job with the cloth partly smoothed out and partly full of wrinkles and the resin setting up fast.

On smaller areas that you can handle quickly and on vertical surfaces, apply the cloth immediately, right after you put on the coat of resin, and finish the job with a couple more coats of resin. After the earlier coats have dried, follow up with a finish coat, which should leave the surface looking as though it has been freshly varnished.

Edge-grained plywood soaks up resin fast, so you'll need more coats of it. If you've been too stingy with it, the cloth will appear grayish while it is curing and you will see pinholes in its weave.

● Very little special equipment is needed, but be sure you have the essentials. Among these, I would include a shop brush to smooth the cloth before it makes contact with any resin, paint brushes (1½ inches wide and up), 3-inch rollers, various sizes of putty knives and squeegees, and wooden stir sticks (again, my favorite is tongue depressors). You'll also need acetone to plop brushes in, to prevent their hardening, whenever you're interrupted. (You get very time-conscious when you work with a rapidly progressing and irreversible process.) Have on hand sandpaper of various grades, starting with number 20 grit for your disc sander to mow down ridges and lumps of cured resin.

For your own safety, use regular cleansers to wash resin off your hands, not acetone or lacquer thinners, both of which can be injurious to your health. And I urge you to wear a dust mask to prevent inhaling glass particles and goggles to keep them out of your eyes.

This is one crash course in fiberglassing plywood, but it's more knowledge than I started with, and I've never had any real trouble. It helps to experiment on scrap before you undertake any major effort, and it can ease the process immensely if you have a friend with some experience who will give you a helping hand.

Some of the Instant Boats require little or no fiberglassing; others are completely sheathed with it, as is the case with those constructed by the Tack-and-Tape method. All these latter craft, however, allow you to set your own pace. Whether that pace is one seam a week or damn-the-torpedoes-full-speed-ahead, Tack-and-Tape boats will accommodate themselves to match it, as you will find when we move on to come to grips with the Tack-and-Tape–constructed Gypsy.

PART TWO

Tack And Tape

Introduction

Gypsy, Nymph, and Diablo—the boats that I am about to show you how to build—belong to the Tack-and-Tape variety of Instant Boats. In the first-developed Instant Boats—what I now call Fit-and-Fasten boats—lofting and the need for any kind of building jig are eliminated. In the Tack-and-Tape boats, building has been simplified still further by eliminating almost all beveling. Plywood panels are cut out square-edged and assembled using the Tack-and-Tape method. This is not only a simple method of construction but one that allows a very wide range of hull shapes.

These Tack-and-Tape newcomers are spritely, shapely little boats—no doubt about it. They can be somewhat more tiddly than the Fit-and-Fasten boats, which have great initial stability due to their flat bottoms. In building, the Tack-and-Tape boats are simpler, but because of the fiberglassing involved, more time consuming. I think that they do not replace the Fit-and-Fasten boats; rather, they extend the Instant Boats concept.

I'll take you through the Tack-and-Tape method step by step when I describe the building of Gypsy, but let's take a quick look at the general process right now. Basically, Tack-and-Tape begins with the cutting out of plywood panels, like the planks in plank-on-frame building. These are shaped to fit together, edge to edge, and are temporarily fastened in place with tacks—which, for my choice, are light 18-gauge nails. The outside seams are filled with glass putty. The nails are then easily removed and replaced by long strips of fiberglass tape, which function as the chine logs. So far you've been working bottom up, but once this assembly is stiff enough you turn it right side up and fill and tape the interior seams. The order of these steps may vary according to the size of the boat and the builder's preference. The result is a smoothly curved hull with a multi-chine form, which approximates the form of a round-bottomed boat in those examples with more numerous panels or strakes and therefore more numerous chines.

One variation of this technique calls for stitching with wire instead of tacking with nails. Working from some plans, wire is a necessary evil simply because the strakes don't fit together snugly enough to form an honest-to-God hull. With Phil's plans they do, so you're spared the need to drill holes to lead the wire through and you don't have to wreck your hands twisting the

29

ends together. When I say *evil*, I mean it. I hate working with wire.

Either way, it's still a forgiving method, and gaps as wide as a quarter inch are acceptable. I've been assigned responsibility for helping ensure that any gaps fall well inside that limit. When I get Phil's drawings for a Tack-and-Tape boat, the shape of every strake or panel is clearly drawn, with one exception. That's the bilge strake, which, because of its location, must carry a greater twist than any other strake. (See the drawings of Gypsy on page 36.) Phil knows that only after laying the rest of the strakes is it possible to determine the exact shape required to close up the hull with this "shutter strake," as it is called in yards that build large wooden vessels.

What he sends me includes side patterns, mold stations, the bottom panel, and the patterns for stem and transom. When I have assembled these elements, I make a template out of pieces of plywood scrap fitted to the edges of the side panel and the bottom panel and to the outside edges of the stem and transom. When I have fitted this template to lie against all points of contact without forcing it in any way, I know that it accurately represents the shape of the bilge strake. I remove it and lay it flat on a sheet of plywood, then I take measurements at 1-foot intervals from which to produce the required curves, top and bottom, of the bilge strake and its two end cuts.

I then reduce the measurements to whatever scale Phil has used on his drawing, make a pattern for the bilge strake, and send it to him. He inks it nice and neat right on the plans so the builder can scale it back up to full size.

Now, this oddly shaped strake doesn't look like much when it has been cut out and laid flat on your shop floor, but I know from experience that the budding builder will look at it in wonder when he or she has fastened it in place and it has generated a lovely plank line any builder can be proud of. I remember my own moment of excitement the first time I achieved this effect—a moment I relived vicariously through the reaction of a good friend of mine whom I was helping build a boat to one of Phil's designs.

At the magical moment he stepped back, overwhelmed by the transformation he had just achieved, and stared silently for several minutes. Then he burst out with "By God, she *is* a boat!"

I recently received a letter that expresses the typical doubt about the two-dimensional drawing on a set of my plans. "The drawing shows a good amount of bottom rocker and plenty of sheer. Isn't there something wrong with the plans? The side pattern doesn't show even a hint of this shape. How come?"

My best answer to this is that when it is bent, wood works in mysterious ways its wonders to perform. No matter how any individual part of an Instant Boat may look in the drawings, what Phil Bolger puts on paper, you can make good in wood. What you see on the plans is what you get.

CHAPTER FOUR

Building Gypsy The Easy Way

I strongly recommend that before you build this versatile craft full size, you begin by building a scale model. You can do this quickly, easily, and at next to zero cost, and it will pay off handsomely in the improved understanding you'll bring to her full-size construction. In the most practical terms, it will greatly reduce the risk of having to buy wood twice because of spoilage.

This is what I did, because my decades of boatbuilding experience notwithstanding, I had had exactly none in building by the Tack-and-Tape method.

While you're thinking that over, start familiarizing yourself with the plans of Gypsy reproduced in this book. You can't scale directly off these of course, because they've been reduced in size, but all the measurements are there. Theoretically, if your eyesight and your patience are up to it, you could build a boat from any of the plans included in these pages.

In actual practice, though, any professional boatbuilder would insist on using the three 22-by-34-inch sheets of the actual building plans. They are easy on the eyes, and you can lay your scale rule directly on them to check an indicated measurement or to measure any dimension that isn't specifically labeled. By studying these plans, comfortably nested wherever you feel free of distractions, you can build this boat in your head and forestall any surprises, instead of collapsing into your

Moaning Chair (which, according to designer-builder Howard Chapelle, every boatbuilder should have conveniently at hand) with the despairing cry of "Why didn't I see *that* coming?"

You will be doubly protected against such unsettling surprises when you have completed a miniature version. In the process you will come to understand just how these flat pieces, when they are lined up and bent into place, can suddenly spell "boat." In addition, you will have something you can pick up in your hands and study from all angles.

You can build your model out of cardboard or step it up to mantlepiece status by making it of 1/16-inch clear pine, cedar strips, or most any kind of thin wood you have around your shop. You can produce these thin strips with a planer blade in your table saw; if your saw doesn't allow such close tolerances, then make them a little thicker and sand them down. If you stick to cardboard, you'll need very little in the way of tools or materials. A pair of scissors, some quick-setting glue, common pins to hold pieces together temporarily, a few sheets of drafting paper, and any common ruler will do the trick.

The more demanding wooden model, in addition to the above, would be helped along by a small modeler's block plane, an X-acto modeler's saw (a miniature back-

Completed models of (left to right)
Gypsy, Diablo, and Nymph.

saw with extremely fine teeth), fingernail emery boards to use on end grain and for very close fitting, and a bandsaw or small scroll saw to complete the inventory for the fussiest workman.

Whether you're using wood or cardboard, there are various ways of tackling this project. You can lay your see-through drafting paper right over the plans and then transfer the outlines to your material or paste them directly on it before you cut out the components. If you have access to those thin straight-edged veneers model-airplane makers use, you can lay off all the shapes on the veneers with a rule, batten, and square. I've tried all the methods I've mentioned, building up my display of Tack-and-Tape boat models, and this is the slowest—also the most prone to error.

The quickest and easiest way, which naturally is my favorite, hardly calls for taking a rule out of your pocket. All you do is cut the components right out of the plans with scissors or a razor blade, then trace around them on whatever material you are using. This costs me nothing, as I can print my own plans from the originals Phil Bolger sends me. You might not want to sacrifice a set and might prefer the drafting paper approach.

Though the process of building the model and building Gypsy full size are much the same in terms of cutting out the pieces and assembling them, the model does depart from the plans as far as the interior is concerned.

Begin by cutting out a backbone profile that includes the entire hull, tracing around her sheer, stem, bottom, and transom. Obviously, this centerline template

doesn't exist in the boat itself. In the model, however, it serves as the structural member to which you fasten all the other components, so it should be substantial—either a strong $\frac{1}{16}$-inch thickness of wood or very stiff cardboard. Draw vertical lines on this profile, one for each of the four stations where the frame molds are indicated, and cut down on the profile from the sheer line to half the depth of each frame mold so you will be able to insert the four bulkheads. At this stage you can sand a rough bevel on each side of the stem, on which the side and bilge panels will land, and if you want to be really fussy about it, cut the thickness of the transom away from the profile on the aft end. You can also cut the thickness of the bottom plank from the bottom of the centerline template, to be still closer to perfection.

Now cut out the transom and a transverse bulkhead for each frame mold. All you need to trace for these transverse elements is what you see in the body or end-on view—the width and depth of each frame mold to the inside of the planking (on the plan, the dashed lines show the outside of the planking). Don't cut out the limber holes, leave corners wherever they occur, and draw the centerline on both faces of the bulkheads.

Next, slot all bulkheads right on the centerline, half the distance up from their bottom edges, and slip these into position at their locations on the profile, so that the joining of the two slots places the tops of the bulkheads right on the sheer and their lower edges where they will meet the bottom planking.

Then turn your model's skeleton upside down, glue the transom in place across its stern, and let it set up before you apply the planking.

Right above the profile view on Gypsy's plans you'll find her bottom, her bilge panels, and her side panels. Cut out the bottom panel, being sure to mark its centerline and the frame mold locations.

Cut out two bilge panels following the one you see on the plans. Mark the mold locations on the side panels and cut them out, and you've got all your parts.

A word of caution: The side panels are long and narrow, so when you place your paper pattern on the wood or cardboard, stretch it and smooth out any wrinkles before you trace around it. Now you're ready to close Gypsy in.

Pin her side panels to her transom, then pin them to each of the bulkheads, making sure that the tops of her bulkheads are flush with the sides along the sheer. Work the sides along to where they land on the stem, and if all looks well, glue them there. Then glue the sides to the transom, adjust the frame molds to make sure they lie at a right angle to the backbone, and glue the sides to them.

Spread glue across the bottom of Gypsy's transom and along her backbone, and apply the bottom panel, checking that its centerline lies along the backbone.

All that remains is to put in the "shutters"—the two bilge panels. Note that the true length is shown on the plans by the dashed line on the aft end; the little extra shown by the solid line allows for trimming if bending leaves any discrepancy, and this holds good for both the full-size hull and the model.

Start laying one of the bilge panels at the transom and fit it as you move forward, sanding a bit here and there until you achieve a seam fit you're proud of. Twist the forward end of the panel until it lies flush with the stem end of the profile backbone and check to see that it lies snugly against each mold. Draw a light pencil line across the panel and the bottom, so you can check its alignment when you're putting it in place for good. Apply glue to the edges of the molds, the transom, and the beveled side of the stem, and fix it in place with pins and masking tape until the glue dries. Repeat on the other side, and you have a miniature Gypsy!

Pick it up, turn it around, look at it from all angles. Gloat over it awhile, it will do you good.

Striking the waterline the easy way on the full-size Gypsy. You'll want to refer back to this drawing from the next chapter.

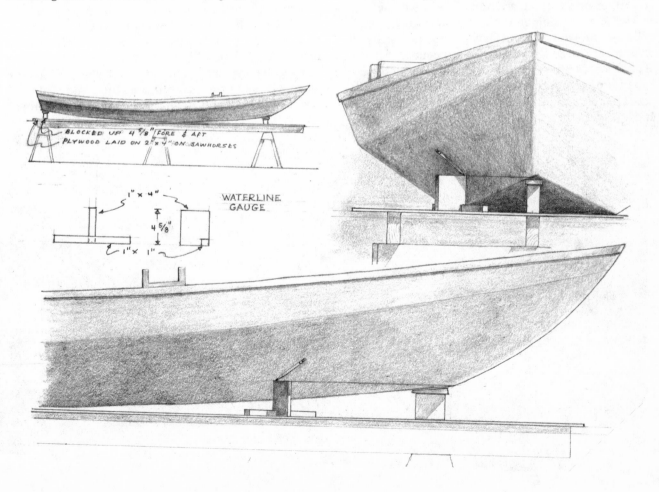

I think I can hear you saying to yourself, "Wouldn't it be nice if it had a waterline?" If not, I'll say it for you, and let's do it—easily, quickly, and accurately. And in the process, you'll learn how to do it just as easily on the full-size Gypsy when you've finished her.

Examine the body view of Gypsy just to the right of her profile view on the plans. This is the see-through view from which you took the patterns for the transverse bulkheads, using the drawings of the frame molds. Note that her waterline touches the underside of her planking at bow and stern, establishing those two points as the ends of her waterline.

Cut a block of wood three or four inches long by a couple of inches wide. The thickness of the block should represent the distance from her waterline to her bottom at midsection. (On the full-size Gypsy, you'll find that distance is 4⅝ inches.)

Place your Gypsy model right side up on any flat, smooth surface, such as a kitchen table. With her midsection resting on the table, adjust the elevation of her bow and her stern until the thickness of the block just touches her waterline mark on both ends. Weight her down, so she won't slither around, and using the top of your block as a rule, pencil her waterline all round. Perfect, in no time flat, and smooth as a whistle.

This same technique works on larger boats, and it will work on your full-size Gypsy. By setting any hull on a smooth, dead-flat surface (I use a couple of sheets of plywood, carefully leveled), I can scribe a waterline in a matter of minutes, a process that would ordinarily take a couple of hours using the usual carpenter's level and string method.

I'm a little embarrassed to tell you that I never thought of doing it this way, in my 30-plus years of boatbuilding, until I made this model. At the same time, I can somewhat smugly report that on a recent visit to an apprentice boatbuilders' school, I watched a couple of students laboriously putting the waterline on a lapstrake peapod, and they obviously had never been taught this easy way either.

For slab-sided skiffs with almost plumb sides, scribing a waterline isn't a big deal no matter how you do it. But for boats having the deadrise these Tack-and-Tape boats have, and any round-bottomed boats as well, I'll go for this method every time. And to think I owe it all to having made that model....

You may want to paint your model when it's all done, waterline and all. I'm told you can do a good job with airbrushing. I've never tried it, but my work with a small paint brush always looks as if I used a shop broom.

Professional model-maker Jay Hanna lives within a neighborly distance, and seeing his flawless work doesn't help my model-making ego any, so for now I'm content to leave the natural finish of my models protected by a few bursts of clear artist's spray dispensed from an aerosol can and let it go at that. I console myself with the thought that I get to keep the models I make, while museums are constantly bothering Jay to get hold of his.

Now, having completed the model, you are ready to tackle Gypsy in the size you can climb into, sail, and row. Let me give you a hand. We'll build her together.

CHAPTER FIVE

Building Gypsy Full Size

When you've finished Gypsy, you will own a shapely and able craft with a length just under 15 feet and a beam of 4 feet that is a good performer under sail, oars, or small-outboard power. Under sail she will satisfy the demands of the most skilled and critical helmsman; at the same time, she is a forgiving learning tool for the complete newcomer to the art of sailing, and her responsiveness will correspond to the improvement in her skipper's abilities that comes with time and practice.

We'll begin with a compressed description of the materials and processes that go into building Gypsy and then proceed with a more detailed explanation and discussion. By all means, refer to the three drawings for Gypsy as you mentally build her step by step. It's a very fruitful stage, this study time. Don't sell it short. When you have familiarized yourself with what it is you are about to do, and have noted such significant details as the changes in scale on Sheet 3, the expenditure of a hundred dollars on materials will see you a long way toward building and ultimately launching Gypsy.

So let's plunge into the basics of Bolger Design Number 436.

THUMBNAIL BUILDING INSTRUCTIONS

Materials

● Five or six sheets ¼-inch 4-by-8-foot AC exterior or marine grade plywood. Four 16-foot 2 x 4s for gunwales, mast, sprit, and miscellaneous framing. One small box of 1¼-inch number 18–wire nails. One pound·of ⅞-inch bronze ring nails. One pound of smooth-wire copper nails. Two rolls of ¾-inch masking tape. Two pounds of Weldwood or Elmer's dry powder glue (epoxy can be used if preferred). Styrofoam as needed for flotation. A 1 x 6 board, at least 4 feet long.

● For fiberglassing: 2½ pounds of 3-inch glass tape, 2 gallons of resin, 12 yards of 38-inch cloth, and 5 pounds of Fillite or any other powder to thicken the resin.

Layout

Butt two sheets of plywood end-to-end and draw widthwise reference lines at 1-foot intervals as a first

Gypsy, Sheet 1.

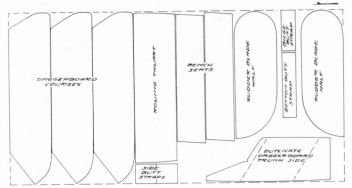

Gypsy, Sheet 2.

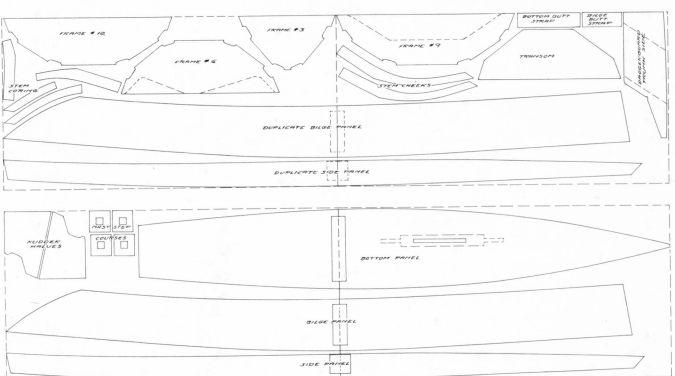

step in developing the shapes of one side panel, one bilge panel, and the bottom panel.

To develop the shapes (see Sheet 1), measure the given distance in from a long edge of the plywood at each 1-foot interval, or, in the case of the bilge and bottom panels, the given distance either side of a straight line struck full length. Drive nails at the measured points and wrap a batten around the nails to sweep the resultant curves. Be sure to mark the frame mold locations on all three panels. Now cut out the butt straps. You want to keep the ends of the butt straps 1½ inches clear of the seams, which will be taped. The

grain of the butt straps runs fore and aft (across the joint) on the side and bilge panels and athwartships (parallel to the joint) on the bottom panel. Glue the butt straps, and fasten them with 1-inch smooth-wire copper nails. Slip sticks under the sheets and saw the parts out with a Skilsaw set square edged (no bevel needed).

Note: Allow the glue to set thoroughly before moving the assembly. In the detailed building directions that follow, I'll give a sequence for the layout operation that gives the glue time to set without slowing down the building.

Bend the nail points over, and using the side and

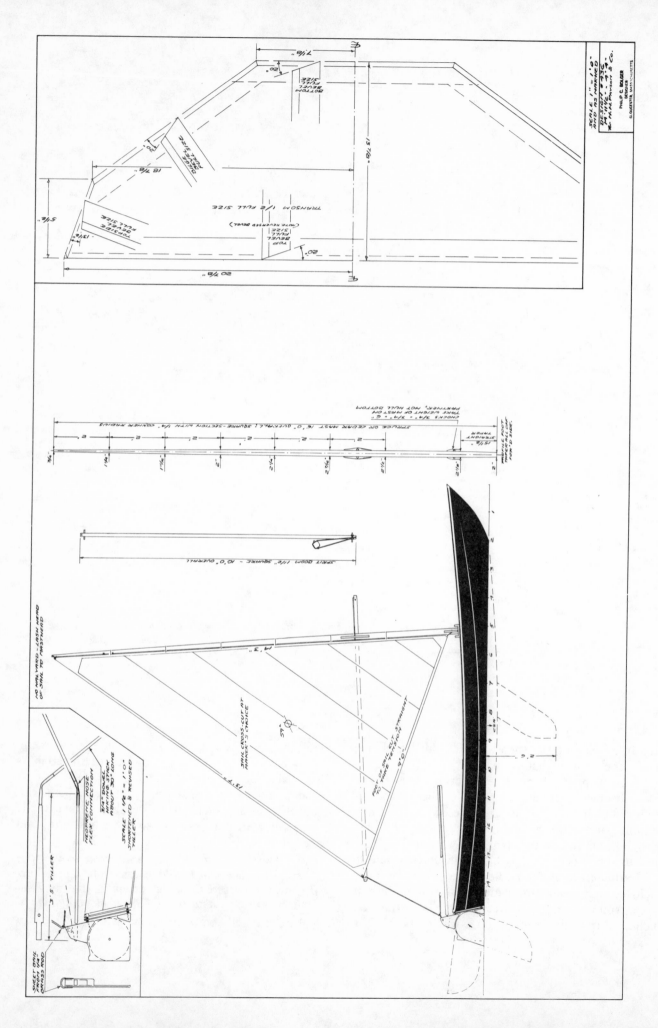

Gypsy, Sheet 3.

bilge panels as patterns, trace mirror images so you won't find yourself with butt straps both inside and outside the hull. Lay out the four transverse frame molds (Sheet 1), and mark centerlines on the forward and after faces of each; the framing pieces will be attached to these mold frames later. Cut and bevel the transom and transom framing as shown on Sheet 3. Laminate the stem from four pieces of quarter-inch plywood, and bevel it before installation.

Assembly

To bring the building process to a comfortable working height off the floor, make a supporting structure out of 2 x 4s, and clamp or nail frame molds number 6 and number 12 to them. (We're assembling the boat upside down.) Nail cleats to the sides and bottoms of the frame molds to catch temporary fastenings driven through the side and bottom panels during assembly. Tack the side panels to frame molds number 6 and number 12, then to frame mold number 9 and to the transom. Glue and fasten the side panels to the transom permanently. Install the forward frame mold, number 3, fasten the stem to it, and fasten the side panels to the stem.

The bottom panel goes on next; match its centerline to the centerlines marked on the transom and on each frame mold, and tack it in place. Put the bilge panels in last, check the end fit, and ensure that the panels lie snug to the frame molds; use tacks and masking tape to hold the bilge panels to the edges of the bottom and side panels. (Use wire if you prefer—anything to hold the planking lines fair.)

Check the seams for fit and apply masking tape from the inside to any seams that glass putty might fall through. Round off all corners, mark a guide line parallel to the seams to follow in taping, brush seams and the area to be taped with resin, and fill seams with putty. Tape seams, turn the hull right side up, take the cleats off the frame molds, and tape the interior, taping both faces of the frame molds to the side panels, bilge panels, and bottom panel. Build and install the mast step and daggerboard case.

Daggerboard Case

Cut a piece of quarter-inch plywood to a 35½-inch-by-16-inch rectangle, slip it down between frame molds number 6 and number 9, and scribe fit it to the bottom. Then mark it for framing as shown in the profile and plan views in Sheet 1. Assemble the case outside of the

hull, glue it in, and nail it from the outside. Fit the seat frames and seat tops, but leave them off for easier painting. Install them after the flotation is put in; the dense, blue, 2-inch Styrofoam available in lumberyards will do.

Outside Sheathing (Glass)

Turn the hull over and sand all previously taped seams free of bumps and glass particles. Coat the entire surface with resin, and cover the hull with cloth, starting with the transom and stem. Turn the hull right side up. Glue and fasten the gunwales with ⅞-inch ring nails.

Waterline

Place the boat on a level surface. Cut a stiff piece of board to 4⅝ inches by 12 inches (4⅝ inches is the greatest depth of hull amidships). With the hull balancing on her midsection, prop the ends up 4⅝ inches above the surface and mark the waterline, using the board as a T square.

Sailing Rig

The mast is cut from two 16-foot 2 x 4s. Saw to cross-sectional dimensions of 2½ inches by 1¼ inches, laminate them, and taper as shown on Sheet 3. Sail is secured to the mast with individual ties (not laced).

- Sprit boom: 1½ inches square, 10 feet overall.
- Rudder: four pieces of quarter-inch plywood.
- Daggerboard: three pieces of quarter-inch plywood.
- Tiller: 3 feet 5 inches by 2½ inches by ¾ inch, cut from a 2 x 4 or board (see Sheet 3).
- Gudgeons: Use screw eyes or make up from ⅛-inch flat brass. Form pintle and sheet bail from a quarter-inch brass rod.
- Snotter: Dacron, ¼ inch by 4 feet.
- Sheet: Dacron, ¼ inch by 30 feet.
- Sail: Dimensions are given on the plans. If desired, a Dacron sail, made up to Bolger's specifications, is available from H. H. Payson & Co., Pleasant Beach Road, South Thomaston, Maine 04858.
- Oars, oarlocks, and side plates.

DETAILED BUILDING INSTRUCTIONS

Your success in building Gypsy depends directly on the accuracy with which you lay out her parts. I can't stress

Gypsy's parts, with the exception of the bilge panel, are all cut out. I had to put these parts together to determine the exact bilge panel shape. You won't have to.

too much the importance of measuring and checking, and then remeasuring and rechecking, before your saw starts biting into wood—wood you've paid for once and presumably don't want to pay for again.

Avoid, for example, the embarrassment and waste of finding out, after you have nailed the transom to the bottom panel and have all your frame molds in place, that you have cut the bottom a few inches too short. Even a fraction of an inch can spoil your day.

Just such mistakes do happen, and at one time or another they happen to the best of us. So take your time. *Make sure* you're right before you commit yourself.

Hull

You're going to start with the layout of the side, bottom, and bilge panels as shown directly above the profile drawing on Plan Sheet 1. When you butt your two sheets of plywood together, tack them temporarily right down to the shop floor so they can't wiggle while you make your measurements and draw your lines. (If you'd like to try scarfing the plywood sheets together rather than butting them, see Appendix IV.) So your floor is cement? In that case, lay down scraps of wood beneath the plywood sheets, preferably scraps about four feet long placed about two feet apart, and nail into them. You may want to do this anyway if you're particular about the condition of your wood floor.

The way Phil Bolger has laid down Gypsy's three essential parts showing vertical lines extending through all three panels at 1-foot intervals is a boon to the boatbuilder. You don't even have to use a square to space them equally. Plywood sheets, whatever faults they may have, are finished as square as you can get, so all you do is mark off those 1-foot intervals along both edges of the butted sheets and draw lines with a straight edge to connect them. It's much faster and more accurate than juggling a square, a pencil, and a straight edge.

Number each vertical line on both the plans and the wood as you go, so it will be obvious which one you missed in case you skip a measurement or want to go back and recheck something.

To develop the shape of the side panel, measure in from the edge of the sheet at each interval, and drive in one of those 1¼-inch number 18–wire nails. (Drive them about halfway in, so you have a support for the batten and so you can easily remove them later.) When you've driven in a full set, take a flexible wooden batten about ⅜ inch thick by 1 inch wide that is long enough to continue a fair curve beyond the actual ends of the panel, set it on the flat, and bend it edgewise around the curve, securing it with small nails as necessary. Sight the curve for fairness. If you see flat spots or bumps, check your plans, check your measurements, and check your batten. When the batten lies in a fair curve, scribe its sweep. You can make a batten from the edge of a 2 x 4 or from a clear pine board—any stock that is free from objectionable knots or twisty grain and will bend smoothly. Note that there are curves on both sides of this panel.

While you're at it, mark the location of each of the frame molds on the panel, and mark its ends as well. If some of the measurements you meet with don't seem to be clear in direction or purpose, lay your scale rule on the plans and check them out before you mark the plywood. Each detail on the plans serves some purpose in helping the builder mark the material accurately for cutting.

Now buttstrap the joint of the side panel, using either a single or double thickness of ¼-inch plywood 6 inches wide. Lay it with the grain running across the joint—that is, fore and aft. Keep the bottom of the strap clear of the bottom edge of the panel by at least 1½ inches. Glue the strap, and fasten it with smooth-wire, flat-headed copper nails long enough to protrude through the underside of the joint. That's why the 1-inch nails are specified in the bill of materials. Don't be bashful, drive them right through into the wood beneath. Space the nails about 2½ inches apart and stagger them across the joint.

While the glue is setting up, line off the bilge panel. The plan shows a straight line running through its entire length, and measurements establishing the points at which to drive your nails are clearly indicated to help you establish both curves of this panel. You can reproduce this line on your plywood by using the measurements just to the right of the panel drawing, which place it 2 feet 9¼ inches below the top edge of the sheet (1 foot 9¾ inches plus 11½ inches).

When you have transferred the shape to the plywood, buttstrap the joint with a single or double thickness of ¼-inch plywood 4 inches wide and 11⅜ inches long, this time keeping its ends 1½ inches back from both edges, as both will land on a seam which will later be taped. Note that the dashed line on the aft or right-hand end of the bilge panel shows its true length—an exact fit to a cat's whisker, provided you make no mistakes. I would leave the extra inch on, at this point, for "just in case." You can always trim it off later if you don't need it, but you'd be hard put to add it back.

Now for the bottom. All the width measurements are taken from the centerline of this panel, which begins at the stem, 11½ inches below the edge of the plywood sheet. Repeat the nails-and-batten procedure, and mark the frame locations and the placement of the slightly off-center slot for the daggerboard. Again, when you buttstrap the joint, keep the strap 1½ inches back from both edges.

By now the glue in the butt joint of the side panel will have set sufficiently, and you can cut the side panel free with your Skilsaw. Then tip it on edge and hold a maul against the butt-strap nailheads while you're whacking the points over and back into the grain of the wood.

Repeat the process with the bilge panel. Because I usually work without a helper, I am always finding ways of doing things as easily as I can by myself. When I tip up a panel, I straddle it near the butt joint, holding it between my knees. This leaves both hands free to wield both maul and hammer. When I was younger, it didn't seem to matter what position I found myself in when whacking the nail points over, so I was apt to start clinching nails at the top and work my way down, so that I ended in a full crouch.

No more. Now I start at the bottom and work up, gradually straightening as I near the top row of nails; I'm standing up when I finish and my back isn't tired. It works.

Next, cut out the bottom panel. Then, using your finished bilge and side panels as templates, cut mirror image duplicates from two more butted sheets. Again: Do make sure that you don't end up with butt straps on the inside of one side of your boat and on the outside of the other. Even a Moaning Chair couldn't get you out of that one.

Sheet 2 gives you the layout of Gypsy's four frame molds. Lay them out full size on the plywood according to the solid lines shown on Sheet 2, and cut them out. Don't cut down frame molds 6 and 9 to the dashed lines (Sheet 2)—for now, you need the whole shape for stiffness. And don't put the framing pieces (pieces of reinforcing lumber) on your frame molds yet, because you don't want them interfering with glass-taping the molds into place. For now, just draw centerlines on both faces of each frame mold, and mark the locations of the framing pieces according to Sheet 1, so the pieces can be cut and beveled later.

Still on Sheet 1, down in its right-hand corner you will see a cross-sectional view of the seams. Make a pattern for the limber holes and cut them out of the frame molds with a sabersaw.

Sheet 3, which shows Gypsy's sail plan, also shows her transom dimensions. Draw it full size on the plywood according to the scheme shown on Sheet 2, and cut it out square edged, then cut the bevels.

I'd go the same route with the transom framing pieces—cut them square edged, 2 inches wide or a little wider to start with in order to finish them to 1½ inches when beveled. (Framing pieces are got out of 2 x 4s.) Then install the beveled framing pieces on the beveled transom. Do not try nailing a square-cut framing piece to a square-cut transom with the idea of beveling them

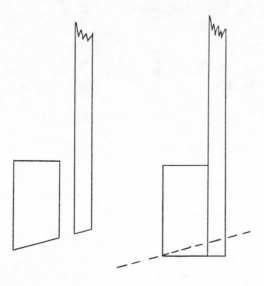

Bevel transom framing or the framing pieces on the frame molds separately, before fastening them to the plywood, as at left. If the transom or frame mold and its framing pieces are assembled square-edged and then beveled, the dimensions come out shy, as shown at right.

Gypsy's transom with its framing pieces beveled and motor mount in place.

both together; you'll come out short. I mention this because just recently I learned a lesson from an irate lady who was building the Elegant Punt—one of the original fleet of Instant Boats. She insisted that the instructions said to bevel the transom and transom framing together, and that as a result her transom was too low. Actually, the instructions were OK. But they were vague, to her, because a full-size insert stated that the transom and frame were beveled as shown. To her, that meant that she was to bevel them simultaneously, after they were assembled.

I don't mean to be critical of the lady's knowledge of carpentry or of her judgment; it was a good honest mistake. It would be nice to be able to offer error-proof plans, but it is probably impossible to foresee and correct every item in a set of building instructions that may trip someone up. I try, and maybe I repeat and explain too much. I would rather err on that side than fail to explain enough.

In any case, glue and fasten your prebeveled framing pieces to Gypsy's prebeveled transom, and we will move along to tackle her stem. With that behind us, we will have completed all the essential parts, and they will be ready for final assembly.

Build up the stem by gluing together the two stem cheeks and four stem core pieces, cut according to the scheme on Sheet 2 out of ¼-inch plywood shaped to the dimensions shown on the profile on Sheet 1. You can use two pieces of ½-inch plywood if you happen to have it on hand (it's not included in the bill of materials). I

used the ¼-inch stuff because I was checking out the plans by building the prototype, and I wanted to adhere to the specifications. It worked fine.

Those horizontal lines spaced at 3-inch vertical intervals establish the points at which you drive the nails to sweep your batten around. If you extend the bottom line 12 inches beyond its 23½-inch length, it will strike the forward face of the number 3 frame mold, and the ¹⁵⁄₁₆-inch measurement noted there means that the stem is deeper than the extension of the bottom line by that amount, in order to meet the rocker of the bottom (see Sheet 3). Make allowance for this.

Just below the base of the stem in the profile drawing there is a full-size view of the stem in cross section, which indicates a ⅝-inch bevel port and starboard for the side and bilge panels to land on. Cut the bevel with a bandsaw or sabersaw, from the stemhead to the bottom of the stem.

As I mentioned in the condensed description, it is easier to assemble the hull if you raise her to a comfortable working height, so let's make some legs for her. At this stage we'll be working on her upside down. Cut four 2 x 4s 2 feet long, two for support under frame mold number 12 and two for number 6, and scab an 18½-inch board to the face of each 2 x 4. The top edges of the boards will fall 5½ inches below the tops of the

The side panels are tacked to frame molds number 6 and number 12. Number 9 is going in.

While the stem is tacked to the number 3 frame mold, its forward end is supported on a block. Forward ends of the sides will be tacked to the stem next.

2 x 4s, making shelves for the tops of the frames to rest on. Plywood bracing added to the bottoms of these legs will keep the assembly from wobbling.

Quarter-inch end-grain plywood isn't much to aim for when you're nailing the side panels to the frame molds, so tack temporary cleats to their sides to provide a larger area for the number 18–wire nails to find.

With frame molds number 6 and number 12 upside down on their legs, tack the side panels to them. If the structure seems a bit flimsy for this setup, tack a board across their tops to stiffen them.

Next we'll put in the midframe mold, number 9, then the transom, and finally frame mold number 3, to which the stem is nailed. The frame molds can be clamped in place until the nails are driven. Bend the forward ends of the side panels in and around, and tack them temporarily to their respective stem faces with one nail each. A Spanish windlass, which is simply a rope around the two pieces that can be twisted to take a strain, will help hold the sides to frame mold number 3 and snug against the stem if necessary.

Before you tack the bottom panel down, tack cleats to the bottoms of the frame molds just as you did to their sides, to make sure the nails you drive will hit something.

Smear glue on the bottom edge of the transom fram-

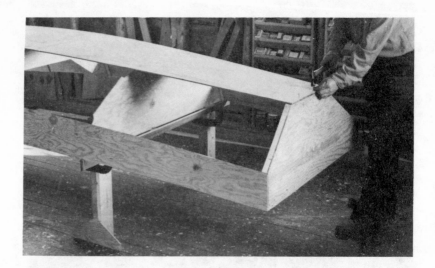

Starting at the transom, match centerlines as described in the text and tack down the bottom panel.

With the bottom panel in place, bilge panels come next. Here a bilge panel is literally falling into place. When a boat is built upside down, gravity works for you.

ing and nail the bottom panel to it, being careful to match up the centerlines.

Now tack the bottom panel to the number 12 frame mold, and progress forward, tacking it to each of the other molds, always matching centerlines. Finally, recess it into the stem. Check again to see how the forward ends of the side panels lie against the stem. If they match flush, then glue the side panels to it and finish nailing. If not, adjust the forward end of the assembly until they do.

You don't need any cleats to nail the bilge panels to. Simply put them in place and make sure they lie flat on every frame. To ease any tight places—which usually cause loose places elsewhere—use a block plane and a handsaw to even out the fit.

Tack the bilge panels to the edges of the bottom and side panels, and run masking tape or duct tape across the seams to help hold the panels in place. Then, working from underneath, apply masking tape to any seams that are wide enough for glass putty to fall through. On the outside, lay down parallel lines 1½ inches from each seam so that you have a 3-inch wide path for your glass tape to follow as it covers the seam.

When you're satisfied that the seams are ready for filling, mix up some resin and thoroughly brush the seams themselves and the 1½-inch area adjacent to them on each side. I omitted this step in the first Tack-and-Tape boat I built and noticed that the plywood edge grain sucked the resin out of my glass putty mixture, which in turn stiffened the mixture prematurely when I applied it, causing it to drag instead of spreading smoothly along the seam.

So wait until the resin-coated seams are tacky, and then fill them with glass putty. Mix the hardener into

With the bilge panel in place, relieve tight spots around its edges with a handsaw. Note that the bilge panel seam on the opposite side of the boat has already been filled. Exact order of work is flexible.

the resin first, before you add any filler. It was not too long ago that I first came across the Fillite powder I now use to thicken my resin. I found it much better than Cab-O-Sil or microballoons. It increases the volume of the mixture about three times, so it goes far, it's inexpensive, and even by itself it's tough.

Fill the seams with a stiff mixture of this goop and let it set up. Unless the weather is warm enough to speed the process, I'd wait at least 24 hours after filling the seams before laying a hand on this work, rather than risk jarring the hull while the putty is curing.

(If you're beginning to wonder about time, relax. It will take only about three days from the moment you first enter your shop with plans in hand until you reach this stage of building Gypsy.)

After the seams are cured, round off all their corners, round off the corners on the stem and transom too, and cover the seams with a layer of the 3-inch fiberglass tape. (Actually, the fiberglass tape could be laid into the freshly applied putty with good results. I let the putty harden first because it makes the corners of these outside seams easier to round off.) Awls are handy for keeping the cloth in place until you apply the resin. You'll need three coats of resin for this job: The first coat holds the cloth in place, right on its heels the second coat fills the weave, and the third brings out the finished or varnished look and completely hides the weave.

Let all this harden up, then flip her over right side

Would you believe masking tape and tacks? The horizontal stick pressing against the bilge and side panel joint smooths out a local irregularity in alignment.

Above: *After brushing the seams with resin, spread the thickened glass putty.* **Right:** *When the seams are cured, apply the glass tape.* **Below:** *Seams taped, boat ready for turning.*

up. Remove those legs and ready her for the interior glassing. Remove the temporary cleats. With a stick of wood 1½ inches wide, once again scribe a line parallel to and on both sides of her seams and on both sides of her frame molds. Pull the masking tape off her seams. I was surprised to find this was an easy job; I had thought that the tape would stick to the putty and that I might have to chisel it off. Having done its job of keeping the putty from falling through any gaps in the seams, it came free easily.

It's up to you whether you glass her long seams first or start by glassing the frame molds, but I suggest you let my previous experience be your guide. If you haven't done much fiberglassing, I'd begin with the frame molds because they involve only short lengths of tape. And no matter how much experience you've had, if the temperature is a high 70 degrees or more and you are working alone, I'd leave the long seams to a cooler time of day.

Gypsy's low sides make any part of her interior easy to reach, so let's begin the long seams with the bilge-panel-to-bottom-panel seams. Cut your tape to match the full length of the seam, and drape it over the frame molds while you are filling the seam. Even if you have help, do only one seam at a time. Brush it with resin, let that harden, and then, using a putty knife, fill the seam with putty. A short length of commercial belting—the flat kind, three or four inches wide by ¼ inch thick, that

Right side up, offering a good view of the legs, which are about to be removed.

is used in saw mills and factories—is very helpful in spreading the putty along the long seams. Its flexibility adapts to the continually changing shape of the seams from the almost dead-flat edge-to-edge near the bow to the ever-increasing deadrise as the bilge panel runs aft. Immediately put the tape right over the fresh putty, and use your piece of belting to squeegee the tape into it.

Keep the sides of the joint free of excessive globs of putty. The instant you get the whole length of tape in place, go over the joint with a coat of resin, and immediately follow it up with a second coat. Allow a little drying time for the second coat before you brush on the final coat.

Follow this procedure for glass taping the rest of the seams. You'll find it easier to do the side-panel-to-bilge-panel joints if you cock Gypsy up on her side a bit, so the seam lies flatter.

Only the stem is left to be done. Dip up a good-sized gob of putty with a tongue depressor and jam it into the crack that runs from the stem head all the way to the number 3 frame mold. Fill the crack on both sides of the stem, up to the radius of the tongue depressor, and then apply the tape.

You might be wondering if what you have done is really going to hold together. I've mentioned only one layer of tape on the inside, because that single layer along with two on the outside passed my laboratory strength test with flying colors: When I drove the rear wheel of my pickup over a sample joint, the plywood broke clean across leaving the taped joint itself intact. But it's true that the plans show two layers of tape along each seam on the inside, and I can't argue that two layers wouldn't be stronger. So double up on the tape if you like, but only on the inside seams. The outside seams get the benefit of a second layer when the overall sheathing goes on.

I'm going to skip a few steps in the sequence now and talk about the application of that external sheath-

The resin has been applied to a short frame-mold seam, and the glass putty is going on with a tongue depressor. Fiberglass tape is cut and ready. The resin-filled brush will be used to smooth the tape in position over the freshly filled seam.

Gypsy's stem, filled both sides with a deep fillet of glass putty and covered with a strip of fiberglass tape on either side.

All interior seams completed.

Begin the sheathing with the transom.

With the boat once again upside down, grind the taped edges and any spilled globs of resin.

ing. In actual practice, that has to wait until you've mounted the daggerboard case. We'll get to that when we consider the various components that make up the sailing rig. But as long as we're on the subject of glassing, let's deal with the sheathing.

For that, you begin by flipping her upside down again. You may wish to brush a coat of resin over the entire exterior and allow this to harden. If the hull is "primed" with resin beforehand it is easier to saturate the freshly laid cloth. The next step is to grind the taped edges and get rid of any glass bubbles that could interfere with laying down the fiberglass cloth.

For this I use a disc sander and about 20-grit paper. You want to get the surface flat but not smooth. The scratches from the coarse sandpaper make for a stronger bond.

Twelve yards of 10-ounce 38-inch cloth will cover her hull completely. Start with the transom. Cut a piece of the cloth to fit its surface, allowing 3 inches of overlap onto the sides and bottom. Mix up a half pint of resin with a half teaspoon of hardener, and brush on a coat that includes the overlap area. Lay your cloth down on the resin mixture, use your shop brush to brush it free of wrinkles, tape it into place with masking tape, and start applying the rest of your mixture. Work from the middle and brush, roll, or squeegee it out toward the edges. On every surface, always begin with a generous glob in the middle of the area, working it outward with whatever applicator you prefer. Even when you're working on a relatively large expanse, never mix up more than a pint of resin and a teaspoon of hardener at a time.

Glassing Gypsy's sides.

When you're glassing Gypsy's sides, you'll find that a strip of 38-inch cloth will reach from one sheer across her bottom and nearly to the opposite chine. Make no attempt to cut or fit the cloth to her sheer—just drape it along her side, brush out the wrinkles, tape it in place, and start in right in the middle. If wrinkles begin to develop, grab the end of the cloth, give it a pull, and proceed with the application.

Stop your cloth just shy of the face of the stem or anywhere along the glass tape you've already put on. This is much easier than trying to overlap the stem. Just bring the cloth to the sides of the stem, then for extra protection, add more taped layers directly over the stem face itself, and more layers along her forefoot where her stem will take the ground when you beach her.

You don't have to cover the entire hull in one day. Wherever you stop, just pick up where you left off. The area along her sheer that you left unfitted, for example, can be left till next day before you trim off the excess with a sharp knife. Relax, there is no need to panic when you are doing any of this glass work. Proceed at your own pace, and as long as you never prepare more than a pint of the mix at a clip, you'll never find yourself racing against time with resin beginning to harden while you're still trying to apply it. When the entire hull is covered and her fiberglass armor is fully cured, sand it down to a smooth finish.

Now you can put the gunwales on her. As the plan shows, they are 1½ inches by ¾ inch in cross section. I would cut them to a length of 15 feet 4 inches minimum, which is OK if their ends are free from splits or poor grain. If not, cut them a little longer, as best you can, so you will have sound wood and the best grain at the ends, where they are going to be fastened. If you've chosen your 16-foot 2 x 4s carefully, you should have no trouble slicing sound gunwales from them. Spread glue on them, clamp them to the hull, and fasten from the inside with your ⅞-inch nails spaced at intervals of 5 or 6 inches.

My first thought when I installed the gunwales on the prototype was that they would look nice if they were mahogany. After all, Gypsy has quite a lot of class for an Instant Boat. So on impulse I did the next best thing with the help of a can of mahogany stain. I thought I heard a few anguished howls from the traditionalists while I was applying the stuff, but the end result was very gratifying. My camera can't tell the difference, even taking close-ups.

Now let's slip back into sequence by assembling and installing the daggerboard case, which should be in place before you glass the outside of the hull. I'd put that at the top of the list of the elements that make a smart sailer out of Gypsy.

Daggerboard Case

The daggerboard is a substitute for a keel and functions as a centerboard to give Gypsy sufficient grip on the water so she can tack and sail close-hauled or on a reach. It slides up and down in its angled case, which is fitted watertight around the daggerboard slot in the bottom panel.

Begin by cutting a rectangular piece of plywood 35½

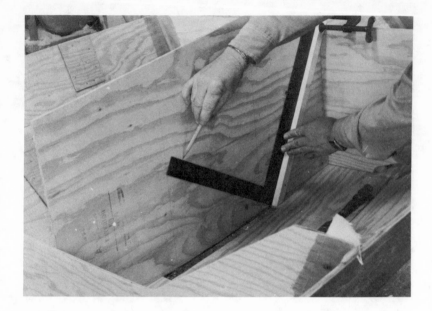

Getting out the daggerboard case. The bottom rocker has been scribed and cut in this 35½-by-16-inch panel, which is in position between frame molds 6 and 9. The forward headblock is clamped in place, and the framing square is being used to establish a parallel line 12½ inches away for the forward face of the after headblock.

inches long by 16 inches wide that will form one side of the case and a duplicate to form the other. *(Note: You won't have enough wood for this if you follow precisely the layout of shapes shown on Sheet 2. The method I'm describing uses more wood than would be used with strict adherence to the layout of shapes on Sheet 2, but the extra cost is worth it.)* Sandwiched between them will be the two headblocks, so labeled on the profile view, which serve as the forward and after ends of the watertight shell that receives the daggerboard. To understand how the final shape is formed and how the pieces fit together, I recommend you give very close attention to the two views of the case on Sheet 1 of the plans, the side view in the profile and the bird's-eye view in the plan, and to the duplicate side of the case or trunk on Sheet 2.

Stand one of the rectangles on edge and slip it down between the number 6 and number 9 frame molds—a snug fit. Using dividers, scribe fit and cut its lower edge to match the rocker of the bottom panel, on which the case will rest. At the top of the rectangle, make a mark 1 inch aft of the edge that fits against the after face of the number 6 frame mold. Make another mark at the bottom of the board where it meets the forward end of the daggerboard slot, draw a line between the points, and you will have determined the after edge of the forward headblock. As the plan shows, a parallel line extended 12½ inches from this edge establishes the forward edge of the after headblock.

If this leaves you a little dizzy—it's easier to do than it is to describe—I suggest that you make a rough sketch of your own, noting the measurements of the

stock used to make the headblocks: framing material measuring 1 inch by 1½ inches. Using your scale rule you can accurately outline the locations of the headblocks and their extensions fore and aft of the daggerboard slot. These pieces will be fastened between the case sides...but not yet.

First you have to apply and fasten the cheek pieces, one to the outboard side of each of the sides of the case. These fit along the inside bottom of the hull and are shaped to its rocker. On the plan view drawing of the bottom panel, they are indicated with dashed lines, and on the view at the bottom of the page, with solid lines as they will be installed in the hull. They must be glued and fastened to the case before the sides of the case are joined together; otherwise, you haven't got a snowball's chance in hell of ever fastening them in place.

Before you do the final assembly, cut the two case sides (trunk sides) from your rectangles, referring to the plan. Trailing back aft you'll note that they're reduced to a small triangle to leave room for the rowing thwart. Their top and bottom edges form a parallelogram, and the forward edge fits smack up against the number 6 frame mold.

When the whole assembly has been glued and nailed, drop it back in place in the hull, glue it to the bottom, and fasten it with nails driven from the outside through the bottom into the cheek pieces—not through the edges of the plywood.

Now apply your glass tape inside the hull around the base of the daggerboard case, just as you did with the internal seams and frame molds.

As you can see from the location of the mast, the off-

Resin is applied to the inner face of one side of the daggerboard case. Note the cheek piece resting on the stool in the foreground. It is nailed from the inside out, which would be impossible after the case was assembled.

The foolproof method for daggerboard installation. The completed daggerboard case was temporarily placed in position, and a pencil line was traced around it. Now pilot holes are being drilled from the inside out. These holes will take the nails when you fasten from the bottom up through the cheek pieces.

center daggerboard is necessitated by your need to slide the board into and out of the case when the mast is stepped. Be assured that the daggerboard will work just as efficiently when it is offset like this as it would if it were on the centerline.

Mast Step and Partner

The butt of the mast fits into a heel collar, and the collar is supported by two longitudinal pieces called step bearers. The outside dimensions of the plywood collar, which is made up from the four pieces labeled "mast step courses" on Sheet 2, are 1 inch by 6 inches by 6 inches, and its inside hole is 2½ inches by 2 inches to accept the tapered butt. The step bearers are made of framing stock, ¾ inch by 1½ inches by 18 inches; they help the collar support the foot of the mast. Install the collar with the after face of the hole 9½ inches from the forward face of frame mold number 6. Make sure to align the collar and bottom panel centerlines.

Mark the location of the step bearers, bore nail holes through the hull from the inside, glue the step bearers back in place, and fasten them with nails driven from outside.

Gypsy's mast is unstayed—that is, there are no lines or wires rigged to keep it upright. This is an advantage in a simple rig of her type, making for a degree of flexibility that will help spill out excessive gusts that might otherwise lay her over. The mast partner serves to provide the required degree of vertical stiffness by supporting the mast at the level of the gunwales.

Get out a board ¾ inch by 5½ inches by 4 feet. Locate its center and mark and cut the mast hole, which will be

Installing the mast step. With the assembly in position, the builder traces the outline of the step bearers. Pilot holes will be drilled from the inside, and these will accept fastenings from the outside after the step is glued in place.

2½ inches square. Lay the partner across the gunwales, measuring 8¾ inches from the forward face of the number 6 frame mold to the after edge of the mast hole to position it. Adjust the ends so that the partner is exactly parallel to the frame mold. Mark the gunwales where each end will rest, and cut the gunwales down so that the partner will be bearing flat on horizontal surfaces.

The word *flanges*, arrowed under the partner in the plan view on Sheet 1, refers to thwartship partner stiffeners, which are fastened to the top of the partner and extend from beam to beam. They can be got out of 2 x 4s.

Before you fasten the partner in place permanently, you'll want to make sure the mast is going to be plumb when it has been lowered through the partner and butted into the collar. Do this by plumbing the centerline of the number 6 frame mold, tipping Gypsy one way and then the other until that centerline is exactly vertical. Wedge chocks under her to keep her from wiggling. Place one end of your level on Gypsy's bottom centerline and the other end on the centerline of the partner, adjusting the ends of the partner until the appropriate bubble is centered.

Apply the glue lavishly to the gunwales, and prebore for your nails (either 1½-inch five-penny fine galvanized nails or 1¼-inch bronze ring nails) so you won't split the partner by driving nails so close to its ends.

Both the partner hole and the mast step hole should be a loose fit. How loose is a good question, and the answer depends on the dryness of your mast stick and the weather in general, but I'd leave at least ¹⁄₁₆ inch all around.

I have a very clear memory of the day that the prospective owner of the first Gypsy, John Garber, came up from Boston to look her over. I should point out that she had been sitting on beach grass at high water, and it had been raining for a couple of weeks. After he had expressed his general approval, he asked if the mast could be unstepped quickly and easily.

"Nothing to it," I assured him and stepped forward to pull it out. And found, strain as I might, I couldn't budge it. Not even the slightest.

Now, having made all the preparations for stepping it, it's time to go to work and make the big stick itself.

Mast and Sprit

The mast is 16 feet overall by 2½ inches square, tapered as shown on Sheet 3. Pine, spruce, fir—they're all OK, as is most anything that is reasonably free of large knots and poor grain. I vote for 2 x 4s I have handpicked myself. Here is wood that costs next to nothing and is easy to come by in most any locality. So it's a mystery to me why I still have so many builders asking: "Where can I buy a stick for my mast?" Any lumberyard worthy of the name has stacks of them.

Granted, you have to recut those 2 x 4s and fuss with them a bit, but for the difference in price between the $6 they will cost and the $70 for a length of Sitka spruce, I for one can do a little fussing.

Let's laminate ourselves a mast and see just what it involves. Buy two of the best 16-foot 2 x 4s you can lay your eyes on, bring them home, and set your table saw

The gunwales are cut away to give the ends of the mast partner a flat bearing. Prebore for the fastenings to prevent splitting.

rip guide at a strong 2½ inches. Saw two slices 2½ inches wide, and cut these down to a thickness of 1¼ inches. You now have two sticks 2½ inches wide by 1¼ inches thick; put together, they are a 16-foot stick that is 2½ inches square in cross section, which is just what you want.

Glue them together on a well-supported surface so they won't sag—either flat on the floor or resting on horizontal braces nailed every 16 inches to the studs in the wall of your shop. Clamp this laminate about every foot or so and leave it clamped overnight or however long it takes for the glue to set.

Look at Sheet 3 again and take note of the widths given for the mast taper. When you laminate your mast stick, the glued joint makes an automatic centerline to which you can apply halves of the width measurements indicated to ensure a smooth, even, and true taper.

Between the foot of the mast and the height of the partner, take the entire taper off on the forward side. If the mast took on a slightly concave shape during the setting up process, have the concave side facing forward, and cut all the taper in this section on that face.

Now, starting from the masthead, using the joint as a centerline, mark off the six 2-foot intervals, which indicate changes in taper. Establish the half-width to one side at each of these points, drive nails, and sweep the taper with a batten. I sawed the tapers on my bandsaw with a helper supporting the end of the mast. You can also do it on your table saw.

With the freshly sawed taper facing you, strike a centerline on it and repeat the process. When you have tapered all four sides, plane and sand the tapers to a

Getting out mast slices of 2½-inch width with a Skilsaw and rip guide. This method is easier when working alone than the use of a table saw would be. An ordinary Skilsaw cannot be used to reduce the thickness of the slice from 1½ to 1¼ inches, however, because it cannot handle a 2½-inch depth of cut.

The glued-up mast laminate is clamped at 1-foot intervals. Alternating the clamp orientations distributes weight evenly and encourages the mast to bear flat on the floor.

smooth finish, then round each of the mast's corners to a ¼-inch radius.

Next, glue and fasten the ¾-inch by ¾-inch by 6-inch chocks, shown fitted to the mast port and starboard where they will bear on the partner, thus placing the weight of the mast on the partner rather than having it on the hull bottom. The holes in the chocks are for the downhaul, which I will explain when we get to the bending and setting of the sail. That goes for the two upper chocks as well, which are about 1 foot long and 1 inch wide (in the plans, the mast is drawn to a scale of 1 inch equals 1 foot).

Finally, drill a small hole—⅛ inch to 3/16 inch—thwartships close to the masthead; you'll use this to reeve a short piece of braided nylon for lashing the peak of the sail to the mast.

The 10-foot sprit is simply a 10-foot slice, 1½ inches square, from another 2 x 4. Slot both ends, and drill for and insert short dowels through each end perpendicular to the slots. The dowels will be useful when you bend on and rig the sail. Sand the sprit to a smooth finish and round off each corner to a ¼-inch radius, just as you did with the mast. This, too, is drawn on a scale of 1 inch equals 1 foot.

Daggerboard and Rudder

The daggerboard is laminated from three thicknesses of ¼-inch plywood. Drawings of these three layers, or

courses, as the plan calls them, are in the upper left-hand corner of Sheet 2, and a bird's-eye view of the finished lamination, drawn one half the actual size, is in the upper right-hand corner of Sheet 1; the leading edge is rounded, and the trailing edge is tapered, with the two outside layers worked down to feather edges where they meet the inner layer. Just below this is a side view of the daggerboard (1½ inches equal 1 foot) showing what portions are tapered and including the handgrips used to push the board down in the slot and pull it out again. There is one of these grips on each side, made from grained wood stock ¾ inch by 2 inches by 11½ inches, both recessed to accommodate fingers.

Drawings for the rudder parts are shown at the left on Sheet 1, including an end-on cross section (just below the drawing of the blade) and a profile view down to the hull bottom on the hull profile. On Sheet 2, the bottom halves of the rudder blade are in the top section and the top halves are in the bottom left-hand panel. This is a pivoting rudder; the lower part can be raised in shallow water and will tilt itself up on striking an underwater obstacle. This pivoting action is illustrated on Sheet 3, with the lower part of the rudder shown in the normal and lifted positions. Back on Sheet 1, the pivot, located at the center of a 12-inch circle, is identified as a ¼-inch bolt set up with a wing nut.

Gypsy's laminated daggerboard is sandwiched between two outer layers of plywood that distribute the clamp pressure evenly while the glue sets.

The leading edge of the glued-up daggerboard should be rounded, and the trailing edge, tapered. The photographs of the rudder construction will show how this is done. Note the starting holes at the handgrip where the saber saw cut will be made. The two handgrip pieces are ready for fastening.

Laying out the rudder. The laminated bottom half, not shown here, will prove no problem. Simply lay out the two laminates according to pattern. One of the rudder's top-half laminates is then laid out as shown. Once cut, it will serve as a pattern for the other laminate. The 12-inch circle establishes the arc through which the top of the rudder's bottom half, or blade, will swing when it pivots on the pin, which is located at the center of the circle. The headblock, the position of which is traced (behind the compass), must leave sufficient clearance for the blade to pivot. To make sure of this, open the compass a quarter inch beyond the 6-inch radius you had previously set it at, and trace the curved lower edge of the headblock as shown. The bottom block position is also shown, traced in the right foreground.

The other structural member of the rudder is the rudder head assembly, which is shown end-on at the stern of the profile view on Sheet 1 and in profile, top left on Sheet 3.

To fabricate this, we'll first lay out the top halves of the rudder full size to the dimensions shown. Then we draw in the headblocks and make paper patterns to transfer their outline onto a 1½-inch-thick plank. The top headblock is made in two pieces, to provide a slot for the rudder, and both of these are faced with ¼-inch plywood. The bottom block is shown ¾ inch thick on the plan, but I made this 1½ inches thick so it would accept the ¾-inch gudgeons I made of strap brass. The plans indicate screw eyes, which would work very well if you can find any with a ¼-inch eye and a long enough shank. I couldn't find anything even close at any hardware store, so I made my gudgeons of ⅛-inch thick flat brass cut and bent to shape, and for the pintles I used a ¼-inch brass rod, all from the nearby Rockland Boat Shop. The inset drawing in the upper left-hand corner of Sheet 3 shows a sheet bail, a hoop of ¼-inch brass rod mounted on top of the rudder headblock, for the sheet of the sail to run through. This works fine, or you can use a short length of copper tubing if you wish; it will work just as well.

Above: *Lay a sheet of tracing paper over the headblock shape as traced on the rudder's top-half laminate, and transfer that shape to the paper using the compass for the curved lower edge. You will use this paper pattern to cut the headblock out of a plank. Once shaped, the headblock is cut into two pieces with a fore-and-aft tapered slot between (see the profile drawing on Sheet 1). This slot allows the tiller to pivot in a vertical arc. A quarter-inch plywood facing piece cut to the headblock pattern covers the starboard side of the headblock, while the rudder's top half seals the port side of the slot. The bottom block is got out of a plank, the two top-half laminates are glued together, and the parts are assembled as in the cross-sectional view in Sheet 1.* **Right:** *Rounding off the leading edge of the rudder and tapering its trailing edge to avoid vibration under sail. Mark off the desired inner edge of the taper using the tapers shown on Sheet 1 for the daggerboard as a guide. Then mow down the wood with an electric plane, keeping the emerging veneer lines parallel with the edge. Smooth with the belt sander using number 60 grit.*

Here again, if you have a good sound sheet of ½-inch plywood, you can make your rudder blade of that instead of a double lamination. Whichever you use, round off the leading edge and taper the trailing edge to avoid chattering. If you have an electric hand plane and a belt sander, you can use these to make short work of it.

If you cut your daggerboard and rudder blade pieces from the plywood as shown, the predominant grain will be running crosswise. I cut these items with the grain running the other way to reduce cross grain in the way of bending as much as possible.

On Sheet 1, the length of the tiller, as indicated, is 5 feet, not including the hiking stick, which swivels on a pivot from the forward end of the tiller. This is awkwardly long, and it has been reduced to a length of 3 feet 5 inches in the inset in the upper left-hand corner of Sheet 3. The revision also shows a different method of attaching the hiking stick (a 30-inch length of ¾-

Gudgeons made from ⅛-inch flat brass, and a pintle made from ¼-inch brass rod. Number 10 1¼-inch bronze screws.

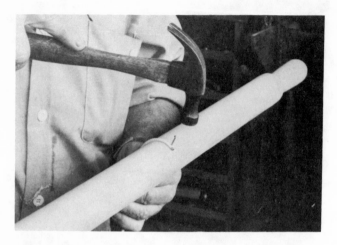

Nylon seizing for an oar "leather," ⅜-inch Dacron for the button.

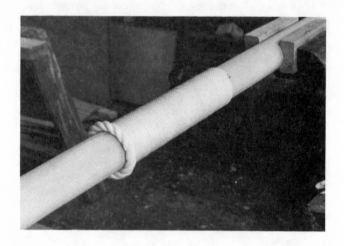

inch dowel), using a neoprene hose flex connection over the end of the dowel and the tapered end of the tiller.

Oars and Leathers

Part of the sailing rig? They certainly are; ask any sailor who has been enjoying a pleasant sail until it is suddenly interrupted by a dead calm.

The plans call for 7-footers, either ash or spruce. My vote goes to spruce, primarily because it is lighter—a quality you will come to value in direct proportion to the amount of rowing you do. Spruce costs more, but to me it is worth it. Partly because of the price, spruce oars are harder to come by; few marine suppliers stock them.

For that matter, ash oars aren't so inexpensive anymore either. And the only ones I see now come already painted in a dismal shade of gray to hide their imperfections. I'm beginning to suspect that some oar manufacturer has cornered the market and is offering a good deal to the seller and not so good a deal to the buyer.

I've also lost my enthusiasm for leathers (sleeves that protect oars where they ride in the oarlocks). I used to use store-bought leathers, emitting continuous growls while putting them on. Another of my gripes is their shrinking length. They used to be about 10 inches long; they're now about 7 inches, which is much too short. You can, of course, make up your own, if you can get hold of the right kind of leather.

Some builders do a neat job of sewing them on or cementing them with epoxy. I tried thin escutcheon pins and had good luck as far as their staying on, but I was never satisfied with the results. Leathers that were nice and smooth when I put them on developed wrinkles later, or their nice clean joints started gaping open. These problems are not earth shattering. But I became fed up with not being able to depend on leathers to behave the same way twice around salt water.

So now I'm using braided nylon seizing—about a 30-foot hank of ⅛-inch diameter to produce 9 to 10 inches of protection on the oars that will outwear leathers. In place of the button—the raised collar of extra leather that prevents water from running down the loom and over your hand and also keeps the oars from sliding out of the oarlocks while you are thoughtfully drifting—I use a piece of ⅜-inch Dacron, cutting it with a rope-cutting gun and shoving the ends together while they're still hot, then pouring epoxy all around it with the oar standing on its blade. When that has hardened, I turn the oar blade up and work some epoxy between the button and the seizing. Then I brush the entire sleeve with a couple of coats of varnish.

John Garber is at the oars of his Gypsy. In 1983 he rowed her from Pleasant Beach to Beals Island, Maine, a voyage of some 100 miles.

On his first voyage with his new Gypsy, John Garber rowed her from my harbor here at Pleasant Beach all the way to Beals Island, a good hundred miles when you add in the necessary zigs and zags, and the nylon seizing showed no signs of wear—only a little discoloration. An occasional rub with Vaseline was all the treatment he gave it the whole trip.

Now a word about wrapping that seizing, in case you choose to go my route. Burn the end of the nylon so it won't unravel, and tack it down to the loom with an escutcheon pin, 1 foot 9 inches from the grip end of the oar. Keep your wrapping as tight as you can (a serving mallet would be nice to use for this, but it's not needed), and finish off just as you started, with the other end tacked down to the loom. The first time I tried this, I tucked the ends under the seizing, but those under-lying bumps ruined the looks and performance of the job.

As for the button, double sealing them as I described above, I've never had a single one let go. Of course, if you are a dyed-in-the-wool rope artist, you might want to make yourself a perfect rope grommet and slide that down the loom into place, instead of using my melted-ends Dacron device.

On that maiden voyage, John Garber found her an excellent rower that tracked well, even without a skeg.

Later in the chapter, we'll watch her being wrung out to a fare-thee-well under the hands of an expert sailor (not me), but for now let's just follow through on rigging her.

Bending On and Setting

You don't have to raise and lower Gypsy's sail—it stays right on the mast. For carrying, the mast and sprit are rolled right up in the sail. As I noted above, the grommet in the peak of the sail is lashed to the masthead with a piece of braided nylon. Examining the sail plan drawing on Sheet 3, you will see where seven more grommets are sewn into the leading edge, or luff, of the sail, including the bottom one at the tack. Each of these is lashed to the mast separately—there is no lacing. The tack grommet is lashed through the two holes in the bottom chock on the mast.

When it comes to securing the outboard corner of the sail, the clew, to the sprit and securing the inboard end of the sprit to the mast, the plans and I part company. At the clew, the plans indicate that the sheet should be led through the clew grommet, with a stopper knot in its end to hold it there, and then hitched back and forth around the dowels. I don't use any

'GYPSY'
RIGGING DETAILS

mast. This keeps tension on the sprit and holds the rig in balance; slack off the snotter and everything is freed up in seconds. While you're sailing, the sprit can swing without binding or excessive chafing.

Finishing Touches

All that's left now is to install Gypsy's seats, seal and paint her hull, and strike the waterline.

You can put in her seat framing any time after the daggerboard case has been completed and fastened in place, but you shouldn't install the seats themselves until you've painted the interior. The plans are sufficiently detailed to make fitting the rowing thwart and side benches a relatively routine operation. You can also fit the slabs of Styrofoam flotation (2 inches thick will do) to their undersides. But again, paint the area first. When all's finally ready, glue these members to the framing material, and fasten them with either screws or nails.

I sealed Gypsy's hull with polyester resin and gave her three coats of marine paint—an undercoat and two finish coats. These aren't the most exacting specifications for a first-class paint job, but they will perform the most important function: adequate protection. Over and above that, you're on your own. Finish her off to goldplater yacht standards if you so desire.

When it comes to the waterline, I follow the same procedure I recommended for scribing it on the miniature Gypsy. The chief requirement is a flat, level foundation for her to sit on, with a large enough area to extend outside her overhang. If your shop floor is not level, I suggest you make it so by laying down plywood sheets.

The only other requirement is a vehicle for marking a given height all around her hull while she is sitting absolutely level, both fore-and-aft and athwartships. This given height is her deepest draft, and you take this from the end-on view on Sheet 1, where it is shown for a displacement of 408 pounds. (Gypsy's hull weighs in at 150 pounds without sailing rig, so this calculation allows for about 250 pounds of passenger weight. She'll carry a lot more weight than that.) Apply your scale rule here, and you'll find this greatest draft to be 4⅝ inches.

All you need do is construct a rigid, plumb vertical, and a base for it that can be slid along the hull, so that as you move it and mark along its top, the height of the line around your hull will remain constant (same idea as with the model).

dowels; instead, I lead the sheet through the slot in the end of the sprit and tie another stopper knot so that the slot bears against the sheet between the clew and this second stopper knot. Simpler, and I think, more efficient.

According to the plans, the thrust of the other end of the sprit against the mast is accomplished by leading a 4-foot snotter line through the holes in the upper chocks and around the after side of the mast, and then using the slot and the dowels to snug it there. I find that this rig tends to bind and chafe, so I still use Phil's earlier system of splicing a sling around the mast and running it through the holes in the upper chocks, with an eye or a thimble spliced into the standing end. The forward end of the sprit has a hole bored to receive a short snotter with a stopper knot on it. This snotter is left on as a permanent part of the rig, and when the sprit has been engaged in the sheet, all I have to do is shove the sprit aft, lead the snotter through the eye in the sling, and belay its running end to a small cleat on the

Dan Segal puts Gypsy through her paces.

This method will work for any small craft, whether round-bottomed, V-bottomed, or lapstrake, and it has freed me from the various stretched-string-and-spirit methods, which to me are abominations. I've never seen it expounded anywhere in any boatbuilding literature. My friend Bill Prosser says he is going to institute proceedings to propose me for a Nobel Prize in the field of waterline determination.

Well, she is ready to sail now, so let's dump her in the water and try her out.

"THE ELEGANT WAY TO GO"

I've borrowed this phrase from a friend of mine who loves to sail. He had been out in his small sailboat and was squatting on the float, making fast her painter, when the owner of a heftily powered motorboat said to him, a little snootily, that when you came right down to it all sailboats were pretty slow.

My friend smiled up at him over his shoulder. "I guess they are, compared with that powerhouse you've got. *But what an elegant way to go.*"

I treasure his reply because it so accurately expresses my own sentiments. I didn't start sailing until about 10 years ago, and until then all my seagoing experience had to do with lobster fishing under power. But that initiation converted me into a sailor—of a kind. For a

while, the fact that I managed to stay right side up and get back to where I started from was all I had to offer to back up my conviction that I was a real, honest-to-God sailor. My performance improved considerably with practice—as yours will, too, if you're a beginner in the art.

Even so, my approach to working the winds with a sailboat has remained laid back. I know I'm not a hotshot racing skipper, but speed has never been my goal. For me, sailing is first and foremost a deeply satisfying pleasure: moving through the water in the most elegant fashion. (Appendix V is written in exactly that spirit. Introductory how-to-sail books tend toward all kinds of discouraging detail. The directions in Appendix V should have you sailing Gypsy in no time.)

The spring afternoon I persuaded Dan Segal to put Gypsy through her paces turned out to be a revelation as to just how wide a gap separated me from a dedicated high-performance helmsman. I first knew Dan when he was an associate editor of *Small Boat Journal*, a slot he was admirably qualified to fill. A little later, I watched him lead the fleet in a sailing race at the Newport Small Boat Show, in spite of the handicap of a broken rudder. If anyone could wring out Gypsy and evaluate her sailing ability, it was Dan Segal.

There was a good stiff breeze that day, and while Dan was petitioning Aeolus for more wind, I was putting in a plea for less. The old god of the winds decided in Dan's favor, and from a nice firm outcropping I had a 50-yard-line seat for an exhibition of expertise beyond even my expectations. He hiked out in gusts, steering with the tiller extension; he quickly shifted his weight when Gypsy went up on plane, and he slipped from one side to the other at exactly the right moment on every tack and jibe. He played Gypsy like a violin.

When it was my turn over the same course, among the other ways I distinguished myself was by executing what Dan called a "death roll" by finding myself on the lee side of a sailful of wind, losing my hat overboard and failing to pick it up in three tries. I was relieved to see it sink, so I could stop wallowing around out there. (My wife Amy recovered it at low water the next tide.)

The second day it was blowing even harder. I rejected the opportunity to set foot in Gypsy, but Dan took my son David out and repeated the performance of the day before in weather as hard as anyone could desire, it seemed to me, unless to court disaster. When Dan came ashore, he praised Gypsy for her ability to get up on plane with two people aboard and said he thought she could stand a little more sail area.

I emerged from the experience with a great deal of confidence in Gypsy's abilities and somewhat less in my own.

The question of sail area frequently produces inquiries from people building from the plans I offer, such as "Do you think she's got enough sail for the light winds we have in Long Island Sound?" or "Here on Lake Ontario we get brisk winds that come up very fast.... Don't you think she's a little overcanvased?"

Right off, let me tell you that you can't change the sail area without throwing the design off balance; you would also have to change the position of the mast. In addition, increasing Gypsy's sail area would probably give her too much of a weather helm—a tendency to head up into the wind, which would mean constant parrying with the tiller to keep her headed off—while reducing it is likely to give her a lee helm, which means she would keep trying to turn away from the wind, causing you to flirt with the danger of an accidental jibe.

It is far better to follow Bolger's specifications for all his boats, as he has designed them to balance under the rigs as drawn, choosing which boat to build according to your surroundings and adjusting your sailing plans to match your skill. If you're Dan Segal, go ahead—take her out in half a gale. If you're me, stick to moderate breezes. And if you're a raw beginner, by all means, err on the side of caution. Remember that none of the Instant Boats is designed for the open sea.

John Garber certified Gypsy's excellence under oars, and Dan Segal stamped her with his seal of approval under sail. I've never tried her under power, but my experience with similar boats tells me that a 2 h.p. outboard would bring her up to her hull speed. Even heavily loaded, a 5 h.p. would drive her very nicely.

CHAPTER SIX

Nymph: A 7-Foot 9-Inch Mind Boggler

Nymph was my introduction to boatbuilding by the Tack-and-Tape method, and she boggled my mind when I first saw her sitting completed on my shop floor—shapely lines and a rounded hull that looked as though her building would have called for bevels in all directions. Yet she drew on the minimum of tools, time, and skill I had ever expended to put a finished hull there. When I put her in the water and rowed her through a lively chop, she gave me a Cadillac-smooth ride to boot. She boggled my mind again when an eager would-be owner bought her out from under me before I had even stepped a mast and bent on a sail.

She still boggles my mind. So here is Nymph, Bolger Design Number 425.

Materials

• Two sheets ¼-inch 4-by-8-foot AC exterior or marine grade plywood. Seven board feet of ¾-inch spruce, pine, fir, or mahogany for the fore-and-aft thwart. One clear-grained 8-foot 2 x 4 for gunwale stock.

• One hundred feet, about 2 pounds, of 3-inch fiberglass tape to tape longitudinal and transverse joints inside and out. Eight yards of 38-inch fiberglass

cloth to cover outside of hull. One gallon polyester resin, with hardener. One quart acetone. Three pounds Fillite powder. One box 1¼-inch number 18–wire nails. One pound Weldwood dry powder glue (or epoxy or marine glue of your choice).

This takes care of the bare hull, or rowing version.

Layout and Assembly

Just as with Gypsy, you establish the shape of the panels by drawing perpendicular lines at 1-foot intervals marked along the top and bottom edges of a plywood sheet. Measure from the top edge to the sheer and bottom of the side panel, as shown. Drive nails at these points and bend a thin batten around them to define cutting lines. Cut the panel with a sabersaw or small Skilsaw with planer blade set just deep enough to cut through. Saw out the duplicate side panel and the duplicate halves of the number 1, 2, and 3 frame molds, and saw out the bow and stern transoms as shown—all square edged. Be sure to mark centerlines on the transoms.

Butt the frame mold halves together, backing the joints with a butt strap of the same material; glue, fasten with smooth-wire nails or brads, clamp, and let

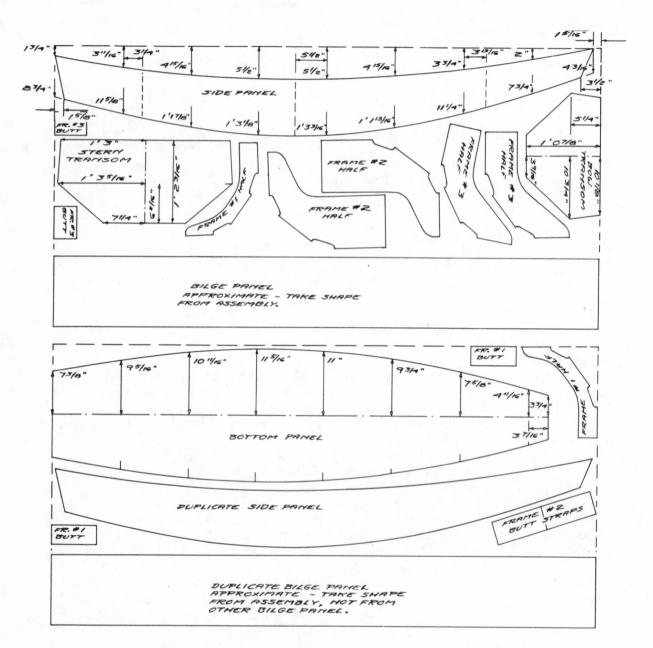

Nymph, Sheet 1.

Nymph, Sheet 2.

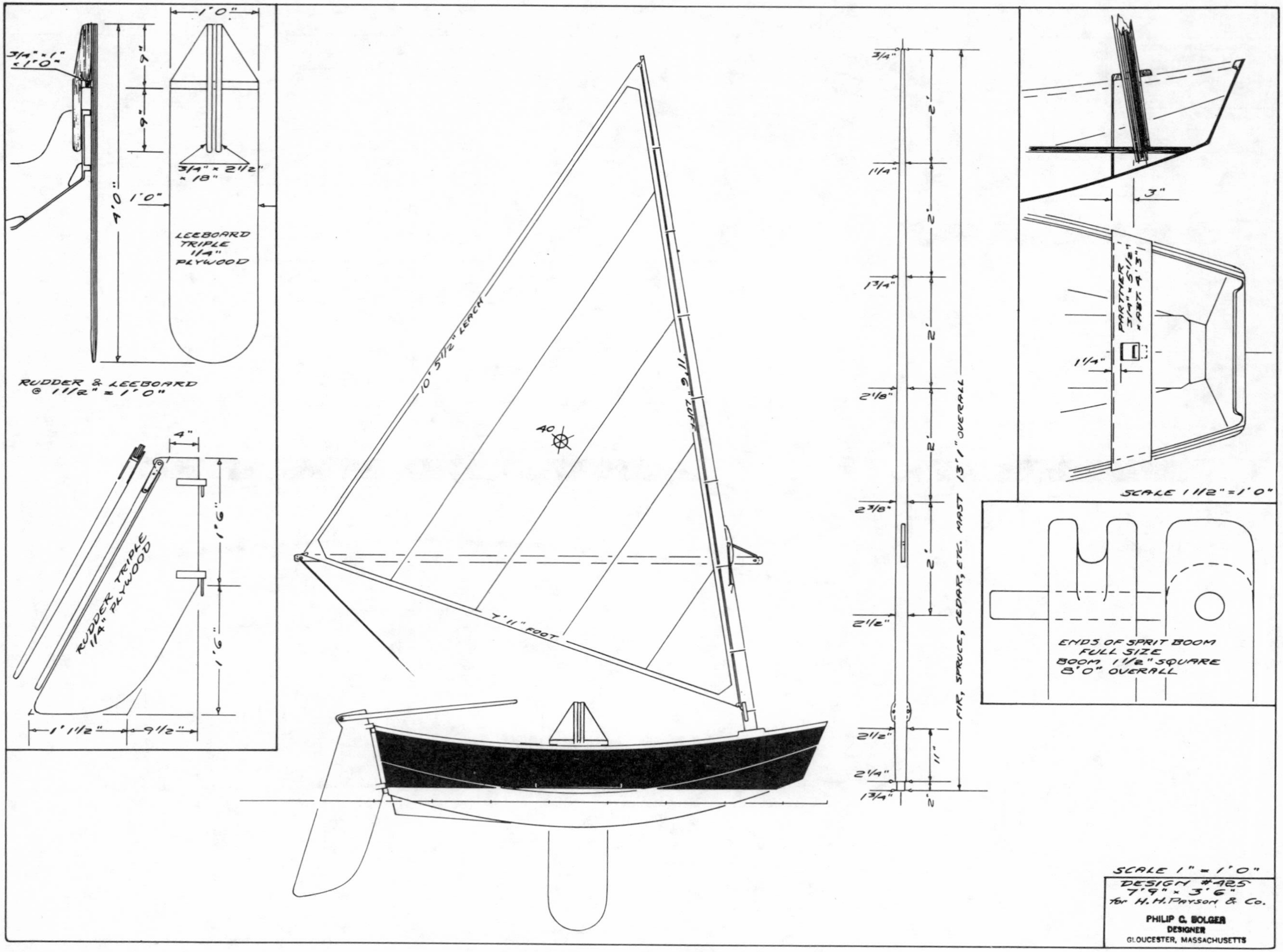

SCALE 1 1/2" = 1' 0"

PARTNER 3 1/4" × 5 1/8" ABT 4' 3"

3"

1 1/4"

ENDS OF SPRIT BOOM FULL SIZE
BOOM 1/4" SQUARE
8' 0" OVERALL

SCALE 1" = 1' 0"
DESIGN #425
7 1/4" × 3' 6"
for H. H. Payson & Co.

PHILIP C. BOLGER
DESIGNER
GLOUCESTER, MASSACHUSETTS

FIR, SPRUCE, CEDAR, ETC. MAST 13' 1" OVERALL

2"   2"   2"   2"   2"   11"   2"
3/4"   1 1/4"   1 3/4"   2 1/8"   2 3/8"   2 1/2"   2 1/2"   2 1/4"   1 3/4"

11' 6" LUFF

7' 1" FOOT

10' 5 1/2" LEECH

LEEBOARD TRIPLE 1/4" PLYWOOD
3/4" × 2 1/2" × 18"
1' 0"
6"   6"
4' 0"
1' 0"
3/4" × 1' 0"

RUDDER & LEEBOARD @ 1 1/2" = 1' 0"

RUDDER TRIPLE 1/4" PLYWOOD
1' 6"   1' 6"
4"
1' 11 1/2"   9 1/2"

Nymph, Sheet 3.

Side panels upside down on sawhorses and tacked to midframe. Other frame molds and the transoms are in position, and the side panels have been sprung into the stern transom with a Spanish windlass. Note the deep-throated C-clamp holding a temporary stiffening board against the midframe mold.

Tacking on the bottom panel. The stern transom is stiffened temporarily with a batten, and an oar holds up the forward end of the bottom panel while the after end is tacked.

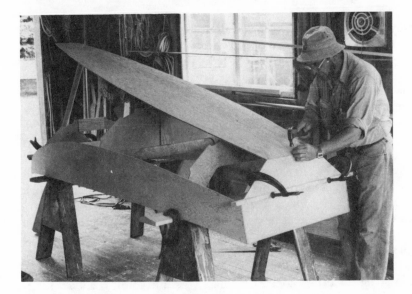

set. Mark centerlines on the butt straps. Bore pilot holes at the frame mold locations on the side panels (dashed lines on side-panel pattern) from inside. Place side panels upside down on sawhorses, butt the midframe against them, making sure the top of the frame mold is flush with sheer, and tack the side panels to it (no glue). Tack small wood blocks at both ends of the panels for a Spanish windlass to bear on, draw the side panels against the remaining frame molds and transoms each in turn, and tack them.

Cut the bottom panel as shown on the plan, marking the centerline on both faces. Align the centerlines of the bottom panel and the frame molds, and tack the bottom in place. If you are working alone, shore or brace

the ends of the bottom. Give the outside of the bottom a sponge bath with water to make it more flexible.

Cut the bilge panels to shape from the plans, bend them around in place, and tie down their ends. Mark them to fit the sides and bottom for final shaping; remove, saw to shape, and replace (gaps of up to ¼ inch are acceptable). Make sure the inside faces of the panels lie flat against the edges of the frame molds. Tack the bilge panels to the transoms and frame molds and to the edges of the bottom and sides.

Glassing

With the hull upside down, use masking tape to cover

Putting masking tape on outside seams preparatory to filling and taping inside seams. On Gypsy the outside seams were filled and taped first, but that order is reversed on Nymph. The reason is that Nymph has no transom framing, and as a result the nails that temporarily hold the panels to the transoms must be near the panel edges, where they would interfere with the builder's attempts to round off the corners. To prevent this the nails must be buried or withdrawn before the outside seams are filled and smoothed; therefore the inside seams are glassed first to bind the boat together. The bilge panels are left long for now, to be trimmed after the inside is glassed.

any seams that the putty might fall through. Now turn the hull right side up and glass tape the inside seams. Begin by scribing lines parallel to the seams at a distance of 1½ inches on each side as guides to laying the 3-inch tape. Mix a half cup of resin with hardener and give the seams a liberal brushing. Add Fillite to the remainder and stir to a fairly stiff mixture. Spread the putty along the seams with a rounded stick or flexible belting. Work off any excess at the edges with a putty knife. Cut tape to the length of the seams, and lay it in the putty. Smooth the tape down with a paint brush or rounded stick. Immediately coat the whole taped area with resin, let it soak in, and add a second coat. Tape both sides of all frame mold joints.

Now turn the boat bottom up to fiberglass the outside of the hull. Get any nails out of the way of the glassing process by either drawing them out or burying them in the wood. Fill the seams, round off all edges, tape the seams, and glass the entire bottom with a layer of cloth and resin.

Further Comments

There it is in a nutshell. Like Gypsy's, Nymph's plans are complete in three sheets:

Sheet 1 shows the layout of the sides, bottom, frame molds, bilge panels, and bow and stern transoms. Sheet 2 includes Nymph's profile, the plan view looking down on her, the body sections seen from both bow and stern, the three frame molds, and a full-size gunwale section. Note that the dimensions of height, width, and depth are labeled alongside each frame mold, and their placement is shown on both plan and profile views. Sheet 3 shows the leeboard, rudder, mast partner, mast, sprit, and sail. Her 40-square-foot leg-o'-mutton sail measures 10 feet 5½ inches along the leach, 11 feet 6 inches along the luff, and 7 feet 11 inches along the foot. Everything I've said about Gypsy's rig—how to bend it on and how to set it—goes for Nymph as well.

There are two significant differences about Nymph as compared with Gypsy: She has a leeboard instead of a daggerboard, and her single thwart runs fore and aft.

The leeboard hangs on the gunwale and side. In case you have horrifying visions of having to leap around the boat, shifting the leeboard (which, by its name, is traditionally carried on the lee side) along with all your other concerns when you are coming about, scrap them. A number of Phil Bolger's sailing designs call for leeboards, and as he maintains, and I can attest right along with him, it doesn't matter all that much whether the board is on the lee or the weather side. I've sailed for hours, tacking as I go, without bothering to switch. Lee or weather, the strain is not all that great, and if someday one of my leeboards should collapse under it, I would count making a new one a small price to pay for my casual treatment of it. (If it ever happens, which it hasn't, I can always shove one oar over the side and hold it there until I get home.)

The longitudinal thwart is one of Phil's unorthodox ideas that has proven its worth in practice. Put a crosswise thwart (the very word is linked to thwart-ships, which shows how firmly based the traditional

The author's son Timothy enjoying a Cadillac ride in Nymph.

practice is) in a small punt or dinghy, and you have severely limited the disposition of passengers or gear. Place it lengthwise and you have maximum flexibility. I'll go for that everytime. It also adds considerable rigidity to the hull.

Back to the speed of building. I started Nymph early one morning, and she was done, rowing-version complete, a little more than 24 hours later. I have to admit that I had several strokes of luck. By noon I had all her parts and panels cut out, except for her frame molds. At that stage, local summer resident Dave Austin stopped on his way back to Rhode Island to say good-bye. He didn't leave until the next day. He had never built a boat of any kind and the fascination of what was going on swept him right into the act. I also managed to enlist the aid of my wife, Amy, always a much appreciated asset, and with her holding the various parts together when that was called for, and with Dave measuring and cutting out the frames while she and I were otherwise engaged, the three of us set something of a record. I think we would make a good team for helping the Bath Iron Works deliver one of their destroyers or frigates well ahead of schedule, as has become their habit.

In making the lengthwise thwart, I ran into one of those problems of progress that so often gets in the way of the dedicated boatbuilder. There was a time when boards 10½ inches wide could be had for the asking, or rather the buying, but no more. I had to glue and edge-nail 1½-inch-by-¾-inch strips on both sides to build a standard 8-inch board (what is now available) out to the 10½-inch width the thwart calls for.

I put the waterline on her the old, slow way, but there's no reason for you to. Since then I developed the method I described for the building of Gypsy, and I recommend you borrow it for Nymph (or any other small craft you may be inspired to build). Simply set her absolutely level and devise a kind of movable T square whose height is equal to Nymph's greatest draft, and you can easily scribe her waterline as you move it around her hull.

If you've already followed the building of Gypsy in detail, you'll remember that I recommended tacking cleats to the bottoms and sides of the frames to give the number 18–wire nails something to bite into instead of the skinny ¼-inch thickness of the frame molds themselves. This advice goes for Nymph as well. As with Gypsy, I would certainly clamp or tack boards across the frame molds, and across the transoms too, to stiffen them before you try to bend the sides around them. That ¼-inch plywood is pretty flimsy when standing free without such reinforcing. Both boards and cleats are, of course, temporary, and you remove them before you proceed with any glassing.

Before installing the oarlocks permanently, the owner should experiment with them to find the best position, which will vary according to the owner's height and arm length.

Nymph had one more surprise for me. That was when the eager would-be purchaser asked me what I wanted for her, as she stood, without mast, sprit, or sail.

I said $400, and then felt a little aghast at my valuation. (I always shy away when it comes to setting a price, and I'm apt to cheat myself if there's no staunch observer standing in my corner.) But then I remembered noticing, a few days before, that a mere kit from which to build a boat of this general size and type was regularly being sold for $600.

So I stood my ground, held my tongue, and watched the man hand over $400 without a qualm.

She still boggles my mind.

CHAPTER SEVEN

Diablo: Speedster And Workhorse

A 20 h.p. outboard will send this 15-footer skimming along at 30 m.p.h., even with two people aboard. To my surprise, adding two more crew slowed her down very little. She can handle 25 h.p. with ease, and at the same time, she remains handily responsive with considerably less.

The source of Diablo's versatility comes clear when you study her plans. With her relatively narrow bottom and her deadrise extending well above her waterline, she presents a minimum of wetted surface when lightly loaded, and it takes a really substantial increase in weight to pull that deadrise down even a few more inches into the water. Diablo will not wallow under any reasonable burden of passengers or cargo, and with her five-foot beam, there's plenty of room for both.

As with Gypsy, I recommend you build Diablo first in· miniature. If you do, you'll find that bending Diablo's side and bilge panels around to the stem won't be quite as easy because of her fullness forward. But it's a minor difficulty, and nothing to be uneasy about. More about that fullness, and why I think it's a definite plus, later. First let's consider the materials and procedure of getting Bolger Design Number 432 together.

Materials

- Four sheets ¼-inch 4-by-8-foot AC exterior or marine grade plywood for side panels and bilge panels. Three sheets ½-inch 4-foot-by-8-foot AC exterior or marine grade plywood for stem, transom, frame molds, bottom panel, and seat tops. One 8-foot 2 x 4 for setup legs. One 2 x 6 for motor support. One box 1¼-inch number 18–wire nails. A handful of bronze ring nails, ⅞ inch, 1¼ inches, and 1½ inches long.
- Two and one-half pounds 3-inch glass tape. Twenty-five yards 38-inch cloth to cover outside of hull. Two gallons polyester resin, or epoxy if preferred, with hardener. Five pounds Fillite powder or other powder of your choice to thicken resin.

Layout and Assembly

Butt two sheets of the ¼-inch plywood together, end to end, and lay out the side panels as diagramed. Mark side panels for frame mold locations, noting that frame molds lie on the after sides of marks. Be sure that the side panels are mirror images. Cut butt straps from the

Diablo, Sheet 1.

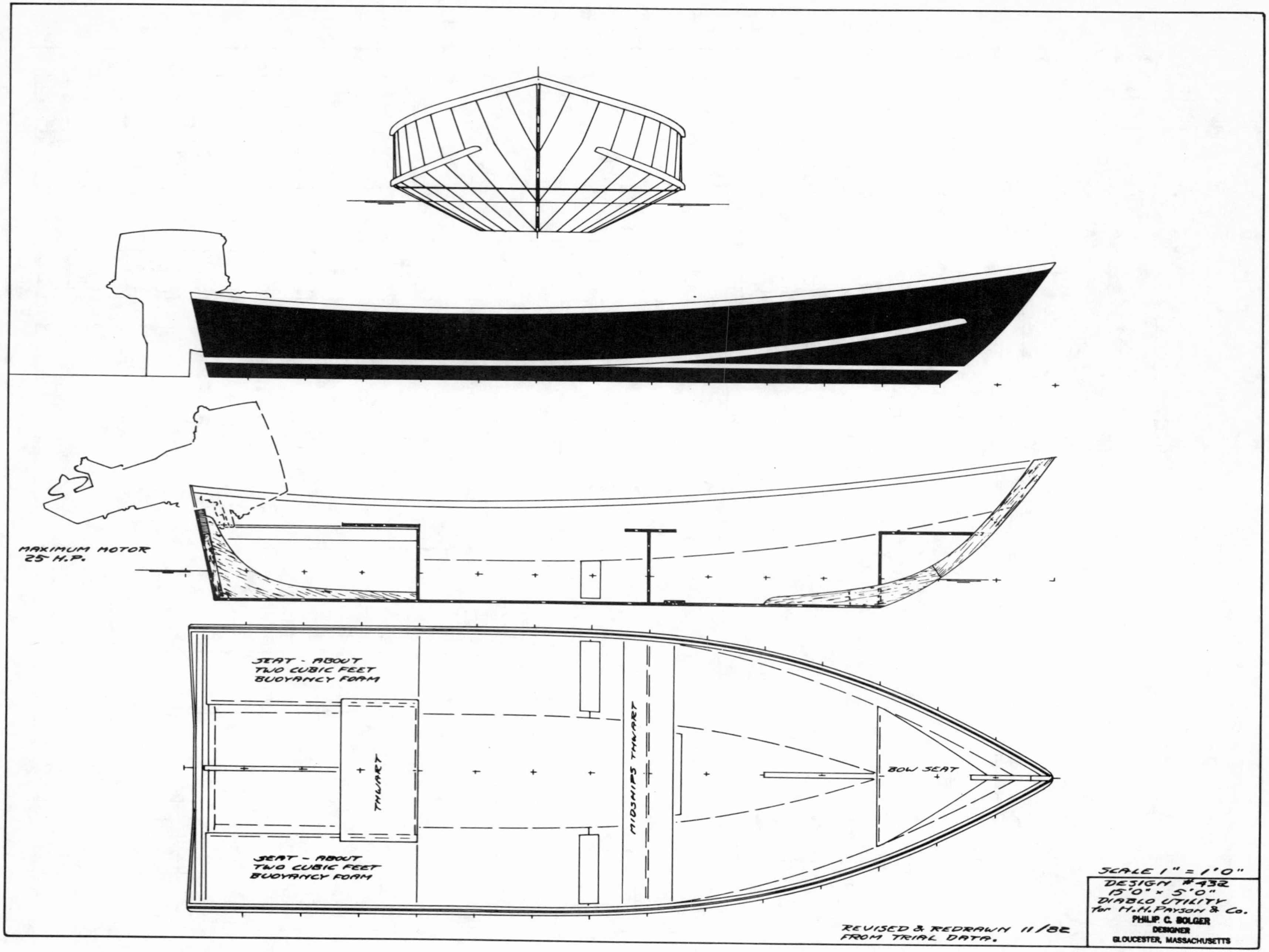

SCALE 1" = 1'0"
DESIGN #432
15'0" × 5'0"
DIABLO SKIFF
for H.H. PAYSON & Co.
PHILIP C. BOLGER
DESIGNER
GLOUCESTER, MASSACHUSETTS

REVISED & REDRAWN 11/82
FROM TRIAL DATA.

MAXIMUM MOTOR
25 H.P.

BOW SEAT

MIDSHIPS THWART

THWART

SEAT - ABOUT
TWO CUBIC FEET
BUOYANCY FOAM

SEAT - ABOUT
TWO CUBIC FEET
BUOYANCY FOAM

Diablo, Sheet 2.

Diablo's parts, except for the bilge panels.

¼-inch plywood with the grain running across their 4-inch width. Keep butt straps clear of sides by 1½ inches to allow for inside gunwales and taping. Glue, fasten with smooth-wire copper nails, and let glue set.

Pry assembly off the floor, slip sticks under the sides, and cut the side panels out with a Skilsaw. Whack nail points over flush with the wood. Repeat procedure for bilge panels.

Cut Diablo's transom, frame molds, bottom panel, seat tops, and stem square edged from the ½-inch plywood. For the bottom panel, butt two sheets end to end; when you lay it out, mark its centerline and install the butt strap (also made of the ½-inch plywood). At one end of another ½-inch sheet, mark off three-inch intervals and lay out the stem; cut two stem laminations and glue them together. Cut the 48½-degree stem bevel on your bandsaw, or use a block plane.

Cut frame molds full height (that is, don't cut them down to their finished shapes yet), so side panels will bear on them when they are bent around. Mark centerlines on both faces of each frame mold, and mark the frame molds for locations of seat tops. Cut the notch in the forward frame mold as drawn on the plans to catch the stem, and cut limber holes in all frame molds. Cut four 2-foot legs from the 2 x 4 to raise the assembly to a comfortable working height. Nail a 19-inch vertical board to each leg. The top edge of the board will provide a ledge to support the weight of the frame molds.

Begin the assembly by placing the transom upside down on the floor and fastening the side panels to it and to the after- and midframe molds, making sure that what will be their top edges are flush with one another. Next, clamp or nail the legs to those two frames to get Diablo off the floor. Slip the stem into the notch in the forward frame mold, and tack cleats or fasten clamps at the bow ends of the side panels to anchor a Spanish windlass for drawing in the side panels to the forward frame mold and the stem. Tack the side panels to the forward frame mold and stem with one nail at each station, close to the sheer.

Now put the bottom panel in place, match its centerline to the centerlines on the transom and frame molds, and fasten the bottom to them. Adjust the stem, which you have fastened only loosely to the side panels, fiddling with it until its flat bottom edge makes a touching fit along the top of the bottom panel. Then nail the stem and glue and fasten the side panels to it. Next come the bilge panels; make sure they lie flat to the frame molds and tack them down, easing any tight spots with a handsaw or plane. Correct any bumps or hollows with additional fastenings.

Tacking the side panel to the stern transom. The bottom panel stands on edge in the background, waiting its turn.

Above left: The stem is ready and the Spanish windlass is rigged. *Right:* With the bottom panel fastened to the transom and frame molds, make final adjustments in the stem position and finish fastening side panels to stem. *Above right:* Bending the bilge panels into position.

Glassing

Round off all exterior corners and fill seams with glass putty. Tape all external seams and flip the hull to tape the interior. First give the fore-and-aft seams a coat of resin, following up with glass putty spread with a rounded stick or flexible spreader. Put the tape into the fresh mixture and smooth along the seams, finishing the joint with two more coats of resin. Tape the joints on both faces of each frame mold.

Glue and fasten the 2 x 6 motor support athwartships, flat against the transom, using ring nails. Cut down all frame molds to accommodate the seats. Install framing for the fore-and-aft stern seats, fastening cleats to the motor support and the after frame mold for the seat ends to bear on, but don't install the seats yet. Put the inside and outside gunwales on, glued and fastened with nails.

Turn Diablo upside down again and sheath the entire exterior with glass. Right her and install spray rails, glued and fastened from the inside with ⅞-inch ring nails. Install Styrofoam as indicated on the plans, install and glass the seat tops, and give the hull interior one or two coats of resin to seal all plywood surfaces.

Waterline and Finishing Touches

The plan profile shows, in contrasting color, the gunwale, spray rail, and a horizontal stripe 3 inches above the load waterline. Set Diablo down on an absolutely level surface. Form a T square from a vertical

Left: Taping the interior seams, using flexible belting to press the tape smoothly into the fresh putty.
Center: Cutting down the frame molds. End cuts were made before the frame molds were installed, because the Skilsaw can't reach the frame mold sides with the molds in position. The forward frame mold has been temporarily replaced with a batten to facilitate interior glassing. *Bottom:* Laying in an inside gunwale. The notch in the forward frame mold serves as a fulcrum for the bending process, and for this reason the forward frame mold has not yet been cut down.

stick mounted on a base that can be slid around the hull. The top of the stick must reach the top of the horizontal section of the spray rail, so that a pencil held there will mark the top of the stripe. Scribe a line on the stick 1½ inches below that, to match the bottom of the spray rail, and another 3 inches below that to match the waterline. Use the top of the stick first to mark the top of the stripe, as you move it around the hull. Cut off the upper 1½ inches, and use that to mark the bottom edge of the stripe around the hull. Then cut off the next 3 inches, and use that to mark the actual load waterline.

Bore for and screw in a ⅜-inch-by-4-inch bow eye 18 inches down from the top of the stem for your painter or mooring line, and your Diablo is finished and ready to be painted.

Installing spray rails. Sticks extend the reach of the clamps.

Further Comments

On the whole, Diablo is quicker and easier to build than Gypsy. I had the basic hull completed by the end of two 8-hour working days; finishing her off occupied the better part of two weeks, working as steadily, if not so intensively, as I had on the hull. I recommend that you set your own pace, and don't make it a race against time. Building any boat should be a pleasure, and the more you enjoy it, the better the boat you'll end up with, according to my book.

I haven't described the building process in quite as much detail as I did for Gypsy. When you find gaps, just check the instructions for that boat and you should find your solutions there.

There are several points I want to emphasize even though I've touched on them above, so this is going to be a little repetitious. Looking at the plan view of Diablo, you'll see that the side panels must keep to a vertical plane from the transom to forward of amidships; the bottom edge of each then bends in abruptly as it approaches the stem. Because of this, the top edge of the panel will try to spring outward aft; plywood panels don't take kindly to being forced into abrupt curves and will not take such treatment lying down. You will need a pipe clamp or a notched board to hold her sides snug against her after frame mold.

Her whole forward section is springy, so don't glue and fasten her side panels to her stem until you are certain that she is in correct alignment, checking that her bottom panel and stem lie in a straight line exactly as shown in the profile.

She calls for a little fiddling in this area, which is why I specify tacking only one nail in each side near the top of the stem. That way you can make any fussy little adjustments to fit the bottom panel to the stem, in particular. Only when you're satisfied that all is OK and true and really right should you fasten the side panels and bottom panel to the stem for good. Then fit your bilge panels on and close her in.

Apparently most builders find that constructing Diablo is straightforward enough because I have sold approximately 100 sets of her plans and have had only a couple of questions fired back at me in return. One was: "Is that ½-inch transom heavy enough? I'm thinking of making it 1 inch." The questioner didn't understand that it's not the thickness of the transom alone that supplies the needed strength. That is provided by the addition of the 2 x 6, which is securely fastened to the transom and extends the width of the transom where the motor hangs on it.

Fasten the quarter-seat tops to this 2 x 6 strength-

Making a stern-knee pattern. To get the outside shape of the knee, put scrap plywood into position as shown and use it as an adjustable bevel square. Then use Diablo's profile drawing to get the measurements for the inside curve.

ener, then add the stern knee you make from your template and you can deep-six any worries about transom strength.

The other questioner had some misgivings about shaping the stem: "There aren't any measurements given for the inside dimensions of the stem. How am I going to be able to cut it to that shape?"

My reply was: "Measure across the stem drawing at several points with your scale rule to establish a set of width points. Drive brads at those locations on the full-size layout you're making, and sweep the curve with a batten." It's the same idea as laying out Diablo's side panels to Bolger's measurements, except that here you make your own measurements. Similarly, you can make your own stern-knee pattern using the profile drawing of Diablo to get the stern-knee shape. The stern knee wants to be 1 inch thick.

In trials, Diablo proved her worth beyond my expectations. She easily carried three people at a much higher speed than I had thought possible, and her performance in tight turns was exceptional—she showed not the slightest tendency to skid. All this despite the short-shaft 20 h.p. Mercury we mistakenly used instead of the long-shaft outboard she was designed to carry.

Phil wrote: "On the Diablo plan printed last summer, the motor drawn is a short-shaft type. This was carelessness on my part, in tracing from the wrong template. Diablo is designed for long-shaft motors. She has a 19½-inch vertical transom that ought not to be cut lower as there is no slop well."

I want to say a few words specifically about the

Speedster and workhorse.

virtues of Diablo's fullness forward. One is that she can carry much more weight up there than a slimmer craft of her size can, and with a following sea that's pushing her along at a good clip, she won't start to nose dive, either. Sure, going into heavy weather she is going to pound a little more, but I demonstrated to my own satisfaction that I can slow her down and wiggle my way over head seas, quartering them instead of meeting them head on.

Given the choice of a full or a narrow bow, I'll go for fullness every time. This bias of mine has its roots in my experience with the various types of lobsterboats I used when I was fishing off Metinic Island. During the late Forties and early Fifties, a strong trend developed away from the lower powered, easily driven fishing boat hull toward a much wider stern with more power.

There was an awkward time during that evolutionary period, before boatbuilders realized that if you put a big wide stern on a workboat and crowd the power to it, then you are damn well going to need more bearing forward to hold the bow up instead of getting it pushed down by the force of following seas piling up against the wide transom. During this transitional period, fishermen were trapped in boats whose combination of wide sterns and narrow bows made them mean to steer with any sea behind you. Most notably, these were the long narrow Jonesport and Friendship models.

Eventually everybody came to his senses, and today big fiberglass lobsterboats are given ample beam and fullness to handle all the power (and all the weight) any owner could want. For the time being, at least, the old easily driven hulls are a thing of the past.

Just before I wrote this, in the course of a visit to the Rockland Boat Shop, Inc., I noticed that all the stacks of molds for the various-sized boats had disappeared. The answer to my obvious question was very succint.

"We burned them all....Nobody makes them that way anymore."

BEFORE WE GO ON...

So there you have them—three Tack-and-Tape boats differing widely in looks, form, and function. The only thing that's typical of Bolger's designs is that each one has its surprises (pleasant ones), and the only thing they have in common is that each one is different. That, and the fact that they work.

We're now going to meet eight new designs built in the mode of the original six Instant Boats. Phil will continue to spin off his new designs, and I'll continue to build them. Through our association I have learned to expect surprise and pleasure. The last time I thought I knew better than Phil what home builders really wanted, I asked him to design a lovely little 15-foot round-bottomed sailing peapod; it seemed to me to be exactly what a good many were hollering for. She is a good little boat, but I've yet to sell a single set of her plans.

PART THREE

New Boats To Join The Original Fleet

Introduction

When we turn to the lineal descendants of the six Fit-and-Fasten craft presented in my first book, *Instant Boats*, we're dealing with a different kettle of fish from the Tack-and-Tape variety. Where Gypsy, Nymph, and Diablo utilize the strength and flexibility of fiberglass tape to tie their panels together, and an additional coat or two of fiberglass over the entire exterior to provide strength and rigidity, these boats are constructed by rigidly fastening flat pieces of plywood using glue and either nails or screws, with structural strength supplied by chine logs, gunwales, and seats (either lateral or longitudinal).

Even though plywood will bend along only one plane, much as a sheet of cardboard does, skillful design permits the Fit-and-Fasten hulls to embody pleasing and complex curves when seen as a whole, except in the models designed for total and simple utility, as Tortoise is.

These boats require reasonably accurate sawing and fitting, but they don't demand any expertise. Most of them call for some beveling at crucial joints, and it would be a good idea to review the use of the bevel square and the bevel board. You'll also find that your architect's scale rule will come in mighty handy from time to time.

I think these boats and their sisters in the original Instant Boat fleet can take their place proudly right alongside the Tack-and-Tape boats. They require little or nothing in the way of fiberglass, and this is their chief advantage for those who prefer not to work with fiberglass any more than necessary. Despite the beveling, they are a bit faster to build than the Tack-and-Tape boats, and I, for one, am fond of the great initial stability the Fit-and-Fasten boats provide. Of course, if you prefer working with fiberglass to beveling and fitting panels and frame pieces, there's nothing to stop you from using Tack-and-Tape techniques wherever common sense allows. The point is to be flexible; using good judgment, alter techniques and materials to suit your requirements and desires.

Some Instant Boats are more instant than others. You can probably whack Tortoise together in very short order, but Windsprint and the Light Schooner will take more time. In every case, however, these designs are based on a series of simple steps. It is the number of such steps, not any built-in difficulty, that determines how long it will be between the morning you begin and launching day. They are all within the ability of any competent user of tools.

If you build any one of the three Tack-and-Tape boats, you will find that you also know how to build any one of these Fit-and-Fasten boats with very little detailed guidance. So I'll present them fairly briefly and comment on each one just enough to help you through any little trouble spots.

CHAPTER EIGHT

The Lug-Rigged Windsprint

The first of the new series of what could be called traditional-style Instant Boats is a lug-rigged craft called Windsprint. But before we get fully into building her, I want to tell the story of her evolution from a highly experimental craft Phil Bolger and I developed in collaboration.

This was a sailing catamaran, designed for racing, that carried a large leg-o'-mutton sail way aft, astern of the helmsman, and a bow rudder right in the eyes of her that was manipulated by a push-pull joy stick and a system of linkages. She had a lee helm—a trait not usually sought after, but one intended to give her better maneuverability and to address her peculiar requirements. We decided that I would build one-half of her— one of her two hulls—and try that one out, using the rig, the balance, and the steering system the complete cat called for. As a single hull she worked, after a fashion, and Phil named her Query. I was too tied up in other projects to complete the whole construction; a builder in Auckland, New Zealand, carried that project through. It didn't live up to Phil's hopes, and no more were built.

But I gained two things from her. One was a system of luff ties that allows you to hoist and lower a laced sail with all the speed and smoothness of the old-fashioned wooden mast rings but with the simplicity of lacing.

This feature is not specifically called for in any of the plans in this book, but it's a handy piece of rigging to have tucked away in your ditty bag, so I'm including a full description in Appendix III. Bill Prosser and I used it on his Bolger-designed Featherwind hull and he was as amazed as I had been when I made its acquaintance in building Query. A pull on the halyard, and this luff tie rides up the mast smooth as silk—let go, and the sail comes down in a rush. It's a typically simple and effective Bolger device, and when I showed it off to a number of respectably barnacled boatmen, none had ever met up with it.

The other bonus I got from building that half catamaran was a hull that I fell for the first time I set foot in her. So I persuaded Phil to design a different rig for the hull. The result was Windsprint.

Materials

Four sheets ¼-inch 4-by-8-foot AC exterior or marine grade plywood. Several 2 x 4s—pine, spruce, fir, or cedar. One pound each of 1-inch, 1⅛-inch, and 1¼-inch bronze Holdfast nails or other type of non-ferrous ring nails. A handful of 1-inch number 14–wire smooth copper nails. Two pounds Weldwood dry powder glue

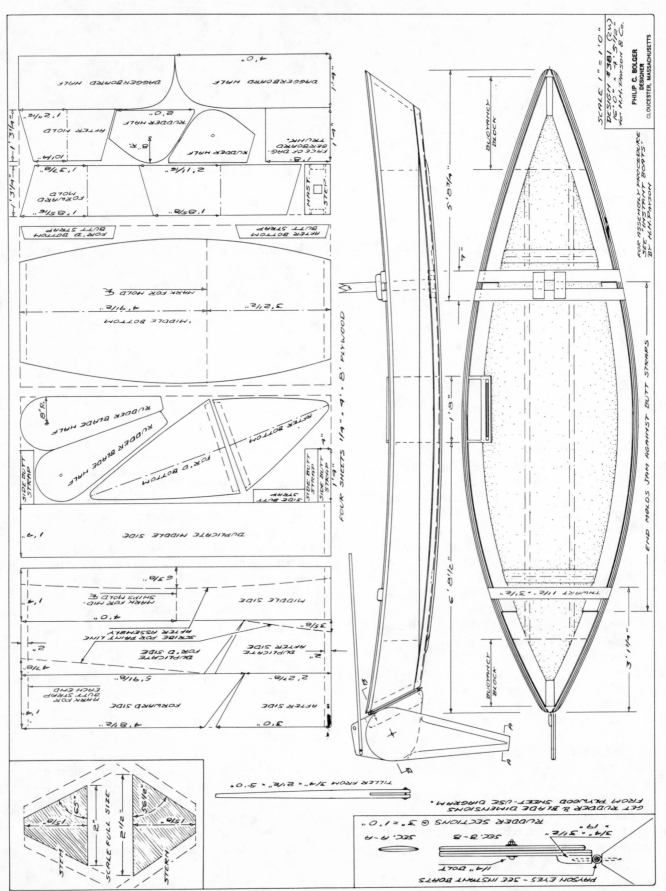

Windsprint, Sheet 1.

MAST – PARTNERS 1 1/2" × 3 1/2" × 8"

PARTNER THWART TWO 1 1/2" × 3 1/2"

GUNWALE TRIPLE 5/8" – 1 1/2"

ALL PLYWOOD 1/4"

CHINES 5/8" – 1 1/2"

MAST STEP CLEATS 1 1/2" SQ. – 8" LONG.

STOP TO KEEP HEEL OF MAST OFF BOTTOM

DAGGERBOARD TOP RACK 3/4" – 1 1/2"

HEADBLOCKS OF TRUNK SIDED 3/4"

DAGGERBOARD TRUNK WELL FACE PLYWOOD 3/4" × 1 1/2" CLEATS TOP AND BOTTOM.

DAGGERBOARD DOUBLE 1/4" PLYWOOD.

SKIDS 3/4" – 1 1/2"

GRIP – STOP 3/4" – 1 1/2"

DAGGERBOARD SLOT 3/4"

1' 6 3/4"

MID-SECTION LOOKING FORWARD – SCALE 3" = 1' 0"

YARD 10' 6" OVERALL – 1 1/2" SQUARE.

HALYARD ATTACH POINT

3' 6"

4' 0"

SLOT IN PLANE OF SAIL EACH END

BOOM & YARD FULL SIZE

112" × 3 1/2" PIN EACH END

CLEATS 3/4" SQUARE

2' 0"

PIVOT ROPE ATTACH POINT

2' 3"

BOOM 12' 0" OVERALL – 1 1/2" SQUARE

MAST 15' 6" OVERALL – FIR OR HARDER

TRANSVERSE SCALE FULL SIZE

STAVES NOT LESS THAN 1/2"

PLUG 2' 6"

TAPER 5' 1"

MAST CAN BE SOLID – ROUND ON TAPER GIVEN.

HALYARD, SHEET, & BOOM PIVOT ROPE ALL 1/4".

TWINE RETAINING TYE

STEP WITH SLOT ATHWARTSHIPS

MASTHEAD FULL SIZE

HALYARD SLOT

1/32" × 1 1/2" BRASS OR S.S.

HALYARD CLEAT

MAST AT PARTNERS SCALE 3" = 1' 0"

TAKE PIVOT ROPE UNDER STOP

10' 6" HEAD

8' 1" LUFF

15' 6" LEECH

113°

11' 10" FOOT

SAIL PLAN & LONGITUDINAL SCALE OF SPARS 1/2" = 1' 0"

Windsprint, Sheet 2.

SCALE AS MARKED

DESIGN #381 (2V)
16' 0" × 4' 5 1/2"
For: H. H. PAYSON & CO.

PHILIP C. BOLGER
DESIGNER
~ GLOUCESTER, MASSACHUSETTS

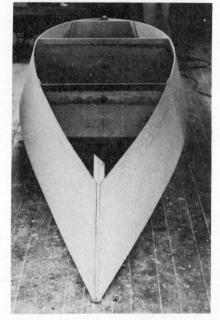

Left: Windsprint's side panels and temporary molds laid out. The batten on one of the side panels is sweeping the waterline curve, which is taken from the plans. **Center:** *With temporary molds in place, sides are bent around and fastened to stem and stern posts.* **Right:** *Fitting the bottom panels. A straight-edge is used to align the centerlines of the forward- and middle-bottom panels. Looks like I cut out the forward-bottom panel before the middle-bottom, the reverse of what I describe in the text, but the end result is the same. The chine log and the laminated gunwale have been installed (the gunwale can go on almost anytime).*

(or plastic resin glue). One gallon International number 1026 clear wood sealer. Two quarts semi-gloss marine paint.

Layout and Assembly

Saw sides from two sheets of plywood as shown. Note that they comprise a forward side, an after side, and a middle side, butted. Make mirror-image duplicates, ensuring that all butt straps will be inside the hull. Mark the locations of the three temporary molds. Glue the butt straps and fasten them with the 1-inch smooth-wire copper nails, clinched over. Cut the temporary molds to the dimensions drawn on the plans, and mark their centerlines. Add ¾-inch-by-1½-inch framing around the molds for stiffness, first beveling the sides of the forward mold framing to 17 degrees and the after mold framing to 24 degrees so the molds will jam snugly against the butt straps. Cut the midmold square edged; no bevel. (Note: On the plan, the midmold pattern is next to the forward-mold pattern, unlabeled.)

Stand sides on edge, bottom up, and tack midmold in place. Raise the assembly about 8 inches or so above the floor at the midmold and install the forward and after molds. Use a Spanish windlass to pull the sides in bow and stern, and fasten the stem and stern posts. Place the

hull upside down on sawhorses. Cut chine logs to length and bevel 15 degrees; trim the outside bottom edges of the hull sides down flat before installing the chine logs.

Next, select the sheet of plywood out of which the middle-bottom panel will be cut. Mark the midmold location and the fore-and-aft centerline on the plywood as shown in the pattern for the middle-bottom panel. Lay the sheet over the hull, leaving an overlap of about a quarter inch outside either chine log. Crawl underneath and align the sheet using the midmold line and fore-and-aft centerline for reference. Mark the shape of the bottom by tracing around the circumference of the hull (pie-crust fashion), and cut.

Rough out the forward- and after-bottom panels according to the patterns, leaving as much excess as possible for later trimming. Now place the middle-bottom panel back on the hull, butt the forward- and after-bottom panels against its ends, and extend the centerline through to the stem and stern posts. Trace around the circumference of the hull on the forward- and after-bottom panels, trim to fit, and replace the panels. Lift the ends of the middle-bottom panel just enough to slip the butt straps underneath it so that the ends of the straps rest on the chine logs. Trim the butt straps to their proper length right in place, and fasten together the bottom assembly. Take the bottom

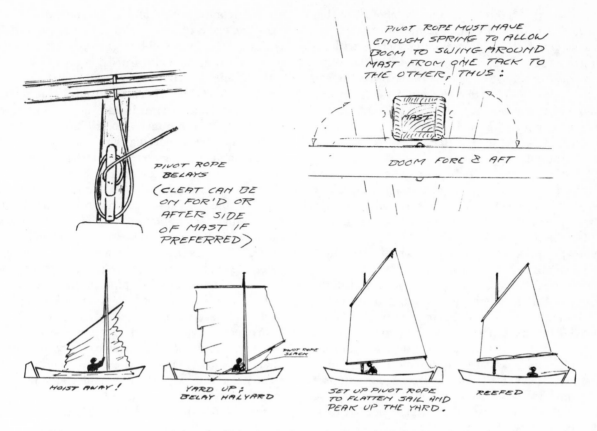

A few details in the rigging and sailing of Windsprint.

assembly off, spread glue on the chine logs lavishly, replace the bottom, and fasten it with 1-inch bronze nails.

Turn the hull right side up. Glue and nail the laminated gunwales, and install the mast partner and stern thwart. Remove the temporary molds.

Daggerboard and Case

You will note on the plans that this boat's daggerboard case is mounted off center to port. Study the plans and refer back to the description of Gypsy's daggerboard and case; the procedure is very similar.

Mast and Spars

The plans show a hollow mast in cross section, but Phil has added a note to the effect that the mast can be solid if preferred—and that alternative got my vote. The mast has two cleats above the partner, a simple one to starboard for belaying the halyard and a multipurpose one to port. The latter has a stop that rests on the partner block and places the weight of the mast there instead of on the boat's bottom. It also provides a guide for the pivot rope or sling, which holds the boom to the mast in shifting tacks. The top part of this device is a simple cleat to belay the end of the pivot rope. Step and partners are well detailed on a scale of 3 inches equal 1 foot.

Further Comments

The offset daggerboard case and the absence of a rowing thwart both reflect the desire to provide an uncluttered cockpit with maximum lolling space for the helmsman and passengers.

Instead of a rowing thwart, I adopted a device I had used on a previous Instant Boat, Teal, for the same reason. This I call the movable seat. It is quite simply a box, open on the bottom and with a slightly concave top. This can be readily shifted to any rowing position one desires.

I want to stress the practicality of raising the

structure off the floor of your shop by about 8 inches when you are in the process of fastening the sides to the molds. If you fasten the midmold in place without raising the sides, when you pull the ends in to the other molds, you are in for a struggle. As the boat tries to take its final shape, making due allowance for sheer and bottom rocker, the weight of the hull will suddenly be supported at both ends, and the middle will hang in midair trying its best to shed the planks you have just nailed to the midmold.

It's a simple matter to find the exact height to block up the middle at this stage: Place a straightedge along the bow and stern on your plan to represent your floor, and measure the depth amidships below that line to establish the necessary clearance.

Windsprint is a very light boat for a hull 16 feet long with a beam of over 4 feet—less than 100 pounds. At the same time, her triple thickness gunwales add all the stiffness to her sides you could want, and her longitudinal skids do the same for her bottom. Incidentally, I used cedar for the gunwales and chine logs.

I wish I had a buck for every time I've promised myself to build a Windsprint for me. (Many other boatbuilders have made themselves such promises about a model they've taken a particular liking to; you have to keep telling yourself that, even if you have to lie a little, just to keep your courage up.)

I had one such hull in Query, the half cat I built, but that went to Bob Titus in Texas. The next was to be mine, but instead it went to Jim Burnham in Connecticut. He wanted to build one with me; I couldn't resist his enthusiasm for a boat I liked so much, so we

started in one morning, and late the next day he headed back to Connecticut with the completed hull. He built the sailing rig later and brought her back to show her off to me after he had learned to sail.

I console myself by going out and counting the yardful of boats I have to choose from, including the 20-foot 9-inch lateen-rigged Instant Boat, Zephyr, which I've sailed every summer since 1976.

You may be wondering why I would pick one of these simple sharpies over a prettier, more rounded boat such as Gypsy. I don't really have a preference for one type over another, but over the years I have taken a shine to the flat-bottomed sharpies because, all else being equal, they are faster to build, they have a lot of initial stability and often more room, and for the protected waters where I sail, they seem just right. And when they're heeled over, they give a pretty soft ride in both protected and not so protected waters.

Right on the heels of "Do you think I can build a boat?" is my second most-encountered question, "What kind of boat do you recommend for my area?" These are equally difficult questions to answer—both involve too many unknown factors. Good, safe sailing depends greatly on the skipper—that and the type of boat probably split honors about 50–50 on that score. Just remember that you can't throw the bull with the ocean; she doesn't listen.

As for ease of building, Windsprint should present no problems; she goes together pretty easily, despite what your first glance at her plans might suggest.

But now, just for a change of pace, let's examine the simplest possible Instant Boat.

CHAPTER NINE

Tortoise — The Ugly Duckling

I first met up with a utility boat of this type in my youth. Woodbury Snow, then called "the King of Metinic," owned a fleet of some half dozen fishing boats, and he saw to it that each one was equipped with what he called "a chopping tray"—a boat like a simple box, able enough to get underway from the beach even in a moderate sea and small and light enough to be hauled aboard a boat and stowed athwartships on an after deck.

One of these chopping trays was my second attempt at building a boat—far more successful than the first one, which my father cut into bits for fear I'd drown myself. This time I worked under the watchful eye and with the helping hand of professional builder Amos Makinen here in South Thomaston. That was a successful experience; it rekindled my interest and my confidence and was probably responsible for the fact that I have been building boats ever since.

Those chopping trays were rather demanding to build in some ways—lots of caulking between pine planks, and steam-bent chine logs. Many years later I asked Phil Bolger if he had a similar design in plywood, and if not, would he do one for me. He didn't answer directly, but by then I knew him well enough to wait patiently until, some time later, what I was looking for popped up from his drawing board.

If I had not already had some experience with a boat like this, I would very likely have been taken aback by the looks of Tortoise. I didn't have to tell Phil she was ugly; he already knew it. Here's what he said about designing her:

It would have made a cat laugh to watch me designing this wee boat, because I kept trying to get more curves into it. Every curve made her more expensive, or bulkier, or took away capacity, so I ended up with the straight lines as the only reasonable way to do it. The profile rocker in the bottom was needed to stiffen the plywood so it could be walked in without adding framing. I put what framing there was on the outside where it doesn't introduce a lot of angles to hold dirt in, and where it gives protection to the plywood. Also, to make it easy to clean, as well as light enough to carry on my shoulder, I made the straddle seat removable.

The decked-in stern was an afterthought to use up some of the leftover plywood. The result is that this punt can be launched dangling from its painter without shipping water. My first trial was done this way from a wharf 12 feet high. Since then, in many launchings off my 48-foot cruiser, *Resolution*, she has always ended right side up and dry. This afterdeck also stiffens the sides, and with flotation gives a little reserve buoyancy for, say, laying out a heavy kedge anchor.

I called Tortoise "Sandbox" at first. I changed the

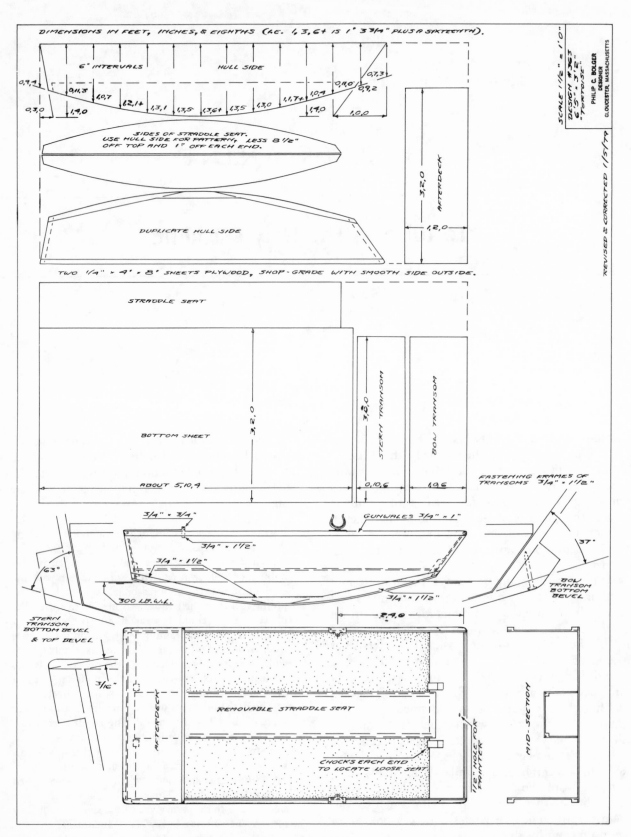

DIMENSIONS IN FEET, INCHES, & EIGHTHS (i.e. 1,3,6+ IS 1' 3¾" PLUS A SIXTEENTH).

6" INTERVALS   HULL SIDE

SIDES OF STRADDLE SEAT.
USE HULL SIDE FOR PATTERN, LESS 8½"
OFF TOP AND 1" OFF EACH END.

DUPLICATE HULL SIDE

AFTERDECK

TWO ¼" × 4' × 8' SHEETS PLYWOOD, SHOP-GRADE WITH SMOOTH SIDE OUTSIDE.

STRADDLE SEAT

BOTTOM SHEET

STERN TRANSOM

BOW TRANSOM

ABOUT 5,10,4

FASTENING FRAMES OF
TRANSOMS ¾" × 1½"

¾" × ¾"

GUNWALES ¾" × 1"

¾" × 1½"

¾" × 1½"

¾" × 1½"

300 LB. W.L.

37°

BOW
TRANSOM
BOTTOM
BEVEL

63°

STERN
TRANSOM
BOTTOM BEVEL
& TOP BEVEL

3/16"

AFTERDECK

REMOVABLE STRADDLE SEAT

½" HOLE FOR
PAINTER

CHOCKS EACH END
TO LOCATE LOOSE SEAT

MID-SECTION

SCALE 1½" = 1'-0"
DESIGN #363
6'-5" × 3'-2"
"TORTOISE"

PHILIP C. BOLGER
DESIGNER
GLOUCESTER, MASSACHUSETTS

REVISED & CORRECTED 1/15/79

Tortoise, Sheet 1.

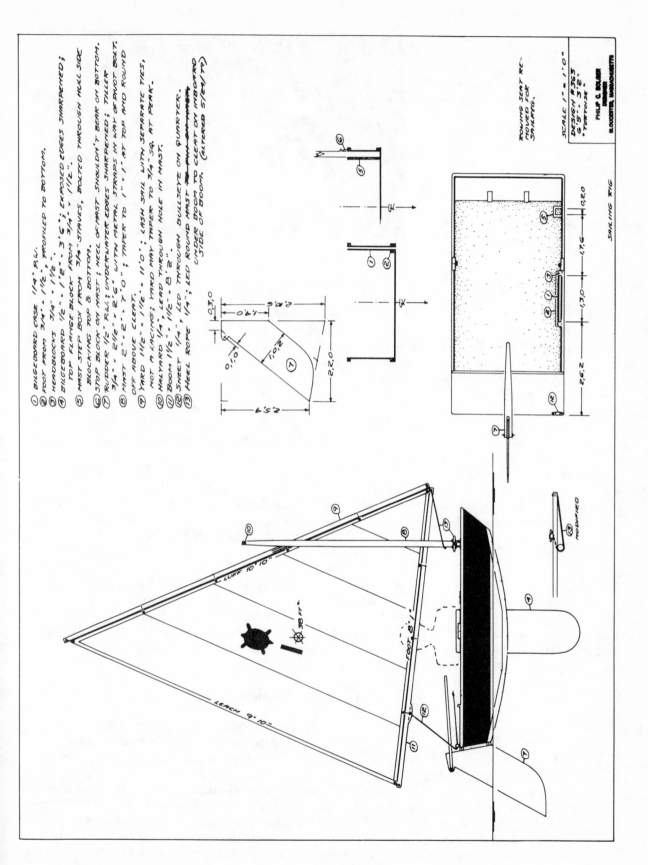

Tortoise, Sheet 2.

Fastening the chine logs in straight sections to the side panels. The bottom rocker curve will be cut next.

name when I found she deserved more respect than I had expected.

I built 30 Tortoises from his design that first year, more as a form of therapy, I think, than in hopes of getting rich at the $85 I was selling them for. I cut out enough parts to make five at a time. The joy of it, and the therapy too, lay in the fact that I could stand there and whack one together without having to think about it much.

You should be able to complete one in two days working at the pace of a Maine native, or a little less if you are used to working in Boston. And without too much additional time and effort, you can add a bit of jingle to her with a mast and sail. First, the rowing version.

Materials

Two sheets ¼-inch AC exterior plywood. Three of the clearest 8-foot 2 x 4s you can get, for gunwales, chine logs, and framing. One pound or 1 quart of Weldwood dry powder glue (or plastic resin glue). One pound of ⅞-inch bronze ring nails. Oars, oarlocks, and side plates.

Building Tips

For gunwales, chine logs, and framing, rip the 2 x 4s full length into ¾-inch-by-1½-inch strips, and cut to length as needed. Lay out the hull sides using verticals spaced at 6-inch intervals and measuring the depths on the plans. (Take the dimensions of the sides of the straddle seat from one of these, as indicated on plans.) Fasten the chine logs to the hull sides in three straight sections as

shown, glue, and nail. Cut the bottom-rocker curves with a bandsaw after the chine logs are fastened to the sides. Bevel the transom plywood and framing separately before assembling the transoms. Fasten the sides to the transoms.

Install three 3-foot temporary stretchers athwartships to keep the sides from flexing when you attach the bottom. Place one about 2 feet from each transom, even with the chines, and the third one amidships, even with the gunwales. Hold in place with thin finish nails driven from the outside of the hull.

Cut the bottom to the dimensions shown on the plans. Place the boat upside down to provide a solid backing for driving nails. Use the bottom to square up all the elements. Slather a creamy mix of glue on the chine logs and the bottom framing of the transoms. Nail one corner of the bottom so its end is flush with the transom and the side is flush with the chine log. Drive nails along the transom frame, then along the sides about 14 inches apart, alternating from side to side (the idea is to get the bottom down into the glue quickly); then drive nails along all four edges about 2½ inches apart. Wipe off excess glue.

Sailing Version

Make a bilgeboard (daggerboard) and rudder of ½-inch plywood or two pieces of ¼-inch, laminated. Cut about ½ inch off the top of a pintle (if store-bought) to make the rudder easier to hang.

Make the bilgeboard case before installing it in the hull, using the hull side to mark the bottom curve. Place the case inside the hull and mark around its side and bottom; use these marks to cut the slot. Apply glue lavishly and place the case on the marks. Prebore for

Fastening the bottom panel. When the after end is fastened securely, the brace will be removed, and with the help of a sponge bath and weights on the forward end, the bottom will take the rocker for the rest of the fastening. The framing pieces on side panel and transom are clearly visible. Transoms and transom framing pieces were beveled separately, before fastening.

nails; nail through the side of the hull to the headblocks first, then nail through the bottom to the foot of the case.

Mast and spar dimensions are indicated on the plan. The sail, with emblem and number, is available from Harold H. Payson and Company if desired.

Further Comments

As indicated, I fasten the straight-cut chine logs to her sides and then cut the bottom curve all at one crack, instead of cutting the chine logs to the shape of the bottom rocker beforehand. I cut out the bow and stern transoms and their framing square edged and bevel them separately before I nail them together.

Tortoise is most easily built upside down on sawhorses. When you're putting the bottom on, start fastening it at the stern, then work forward. You will need a helper to hold the bottom when you start nailing, or you can brace the forward end of the bottom off the floor while you nail the after end.

During nailing, if the bottom seems too stiff, a sponge bath will soften it a little. Make sure before you fasten the bottom that the tops of the two transoms are lined up so you don't build in a twist. Similarly, eyeball the transom tops before you put the stern deck on.

For an investment of a little over $20, the rowing version of Tortoise is an excellent way to start your boatbuilding career.

I found that she rows quite acceptably; even carrying a load of 350 pounds, which brings her down to her waterline, she still keeps her ends clear of the water. She sails much better than I had any idea she might— truly a delightful and very useful little boat.

Timmy Payson sails Tortoise on the Wessaweskeag River.

What I get the biggest kick out of is women's reactions to Tortoise. Maybe it appeals to their maternal instinct—I don't know. But that doesn't account for the fact that men like her, too.

I have two changes to suggest in her plans, and Phil has a couple. The bow transom's top and bottom frames are shown as 1½ inches wide; I made the top frame 1¾ inches and the bottom 2 inches. I also made the gunwales 1½ inches by ¾ inch, instead of the 1 inch by ¾ inch indicated.

Phil's changes are in the sailing rig. Instead of belaying the heel rope to a pin on the mast, he leads it back to a cleat on the inboard side of the boom. He also recommends hanging the daggerboard over the side in the manner of a leeboard, and eliminating the case.

One last word: *Everybody* gets a kick out of watching children or grandchildren getting a kick out of Tortoise.

CHAPTER TEN

Skimmer — The Poor Man's Whaler

I don't suppose Skimmer would win an award purely for looks, any more than Tortoise would. But for the shortest time between two points, she fills a need, and she does that handsomely.

Her total cost of $40 to $50, which represents the current tab for a couple of sheets of plywood and a few 2 x 4s, justifies my calling her "the poor man's Boston Whaler."

Watching lobsterman Don York skittering around Spruce Head Island in a similar type of his own design first aroused my interest in this kind of speedster. Actually he turned out a series of variations. His first effort was perfectly flat bottomed with her forward end turned up like a Sea Sled's; poor cornering and cavitation spurred him to further experimentation. At one stage, his chariot was two Styrofoam logs in a framework bolted to a piece of plywood on which he mounted an old-fashioned wooden kitchen chair. All you could see was Don upright in this chair, tearing across the harbor like a bat out of hell, with water flying everywhere.

It was one of those things people are sometimes driven to do for the good of their souls, I guess. You've got the motor, you've got the materials, you've got the goal. So you do it.

I'm all for this kind of thing, but it's best done with the aid of a designer. The fun of the thing kept nagging at me and kept me nagging at Phil Bolger until he gave up and designed Skimmer.

Even so, I had plenty of critics busy making me uneasy. Brooks Townes, then with *National Fisherman*, kept telling me: "You know, you can flip one of those when you get air trapped under her."

I let Phil know of my concern and left it to him to make the venture safe. When I got the plans, I began to wonder about the effectiveness of the three skids along her bottom. How much lift would they give, and how much tunnel effect would they provide, as the Whaler's cathedral hull does, to let the air escape?

An explanation accompanied the plans, from which I gathered that the combined area of the three 1½-inch skids would produce quite a bit of lift, similar, for example, to human feet, which have performed successfully as substitutes for water skis.

Anyway, during the trial runs of the prototype, my son Timothy drove her at a good clip with his 10-horse Merc, and I could see that she cornered very nicely. When he took her on longer trips, such as out to the Muscle Ridge Islands, he reported that she never showed any tendency to backflip.

Skimmer, and the shortest time between two points.

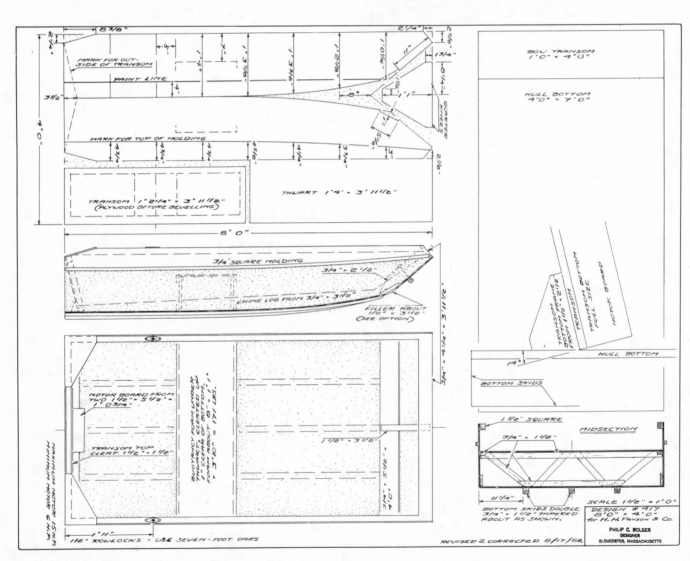

Skimmer.

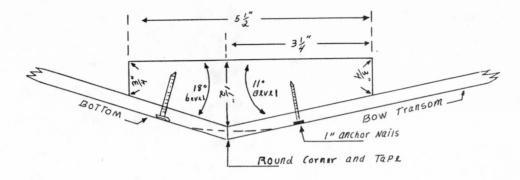

An optional construction for Skimmer's bottom panel to bow transom joint.

Materials

● Two sheets ¼-inch 4-by-8-foot AC exterior or marine grade plywood. Four 8-foot 2 x 4s for bottom skids, inside gunwales, transom framing, and bow-transom filler (optional). Twenty feet of ¾-inch pine, spruce, fir, or mahogany for chine logs and seat framing. One 1½-inch-by-5½-inch 8-foot plank for motor support board and bow-transom framing. A 5-inch board for the bow-transom top framing.

● One pound of 1-inch number 13 bronze anchor nails for fastening chine logs to bottom. One pound of 1¼-inch bronze anchor nails for fastening bottom skids. One pound Weldwood dry powder glue (or epoxy or marine glue of your choice—it's not critical elsewhere, but epoxy is best for the bottom skids).

● Twenty feet of 3-inch fiberglass tape for chines and a short strip of wider tape or fiberglass cloth to cover the bow-transom joint. One quart resin and hardener.

● Oarlocks, oarlock side plates, and ⅜-inch-by-4-inch bow eye. Dow-Corning Sheet Styrofoam (blue) for flotation under seat.

Layout and Assembly

Mark a sheet of plywood at 1-foot intervals as on the plan, and draw in perpendiculars to use in measuring from the edge of the sheet to establish the shape of the sides. Define the curved area near the bow by driving nails and springing a batten around them. Mark sides for molding, waterline, transom rake, seat location, and oarlock side plates. Cut the framing for the top and sides of the stern transom from a 1½-inch strip; the bottom framing is 1½ inches by 2½ inches and is beveled 14 degrees.

Establish the shape of the chine logs from the sides. Lay the sides on the floor and glue and fasten the chine logs to the inside bottom edges. Instead of the filler block noted on the plan, use a piece of 2 x 6 plank (detail drawing of this option is included). Let the bottom and bow-transom plywood butt at this joint and glue and fasten the hull bottom and bow transom using 1-inch nails. Fasten the ends of the plank to the chine logs, plank ends flush with the outside of the sides. Round off to suit and apply fiberglass tape and resin. Fasten the bow transom top (a ¾-inch-by-4¼-inch, 3-foot 11½-inch board) to the bow transom using glue and 1-inch nails.

Mark the outside bottom for the locations of the skids. Cut these from 2 x 4s—six strips in all—and glue them together in pairs as shown, using epoxy. Form the curve either by securing each pair to the extreme outside edge of the bottom before gluing, shoring in place to follow its outline, or by constructing a jig for this curve and doing all three at once. Let glue harden overnight and cut the fore-and-aft taper the next day.

Bore pilot holes for skid fastenings through the bottom, glue skids with epoxy, and fasten them from the inside with 1¼-inch anchor nails, shifting to the 1-inch nails in the tapered sections.

Turn the boat right side up. Install the inside gunwales, sheer moldings, quarter knees, and seat frame. Pack Styrofoam flotation under the seat. Install the 1½-inch-by-3½-inch backing block for bow eye.

The only change I made in the original plans, with Phil's approval, was in the bow joint, which catches the

*Side panels and transoms laid out.
As with Tortoise, fasten chine logs to side panels
in straight pieces, then cut the bottom rocker
curve.*

*Tacking the side panels to the stern transom.
Note temporary spreader batten forward.
The side panels run past the bottom of the stern
transom, as shown, because the bottom panel
extends aft of the transom to add extra planing
surface. I forgot this when I built the prototype,
and after trimming the side panels flush to the
transom I had to do a bit of glue-and-glass
fancywork.*

*Temporary spreader battens are installed to hold
side panels in proper position for bottom panel
placement.*

Outside skids are glued up and shored and clamped in place while the glue sets. Then they will be removed, tapered, and permanently fastened.

lower edge of the bottom, as described in the option noted above. This is simpler and faster, and it makes for better nailing than using the ¾-inch-by-5½-inch framing as originally drawn and adding a filler piece.

There are no bugs in building Skimmer. The hardest part is getting the correct bend in the skids and holding it. I bent and glued two pieces of 1½-inch-by-¾-inch spruce together and clamped them to the outside edge of the bottom to conform to that shape until the glue

dried—one set of skids to each side. I clamped the third set to a jig taken off the shape of Skimmer's bottom. The next day, I tapered their forward ends and fastened them on, nailing from inside while a helper backed the skids up with a heavy maul from the outside.

Ten to 15 horsepower is just right for Skimmer. Don't put on any more, unless you want to scare yourself half to death.

CHAPTER ELEVEN

The Dynamite Sailboard

I didn't name it that—Phil did, mostly because it's another craft (if you can call it that) that I pressured him into designing for me. I asked him for it because my experience with another design had left me with the definite feeling that there was more to be gotten from a sailboard than I was getting, such as better handling and more speed.

So I won't mention the designer of my first such board; I'll say only that the article I saw in a magazine hailed sailboarding as an "Exciting New Water Sport." That was in 1965, and I built one. It was 10 feet by 3 feet with a 2½-inch draft, shaped like a flush door. The ends turned up, and there was a daggerboard just aft of its center.

The mast was a tapered board 11 feet 6 inches tall, crossed by an 8-foot 4-inch wishbone yard or boom. The sail, or more aptly sail kite, looked very much like the old-fashioned kites kids always made. It was stretched taut to the bowed mast, whose foot rotated in a hole in its step. The operator (sailor?) stood in front of the mast holding onto the yard with both hands. He steered by pivoting his body, leaning this way and that, and shifting his weight as needed. It took me a long time to master it, the technique was so unlike any other sailing I had done. Running before the wind was the hardest, especially in gusts, which would try to bend

you forward and at the same time pushed the bow under—and, once submerged, the bow liked to keep heading right toward the bottom. I liked the idea of the thing, but it was slow and less than exciting.

As for safety, the prime requirement was that you had to be a good swimmer, and I decided it was a good idea to wear a life preserver, at least one of the belt types, in case I happened to hit my head in a capsize. That seemed to be the only real danger. I didn't have to worry about the board drifting away and leaving me because the sail was attached to the hull with a lanyard and when she flipped it lay flat on the water, serving as a sea anchor.

Getting back aboard was no problem—all I had to do was roll onto this very stable platform and rest up while I got my courage back to try it again.

I still have it and splash around with it occasionally. Its performance leaves much to be desired, which also seems to be the reaction of any spectators. From their lack of enthusiasm, and mine, I judged that I had got hold of a dull sailer. But when I broached the idea that it was a project deserving the efforts of an expert designer, Phil showed little interest, and the idea lay fallow. Maybe we missed our chance of becoming millionaires because in 1966 *Yachting* reported that Hoyle Schweitzer and James Drake had filed for a

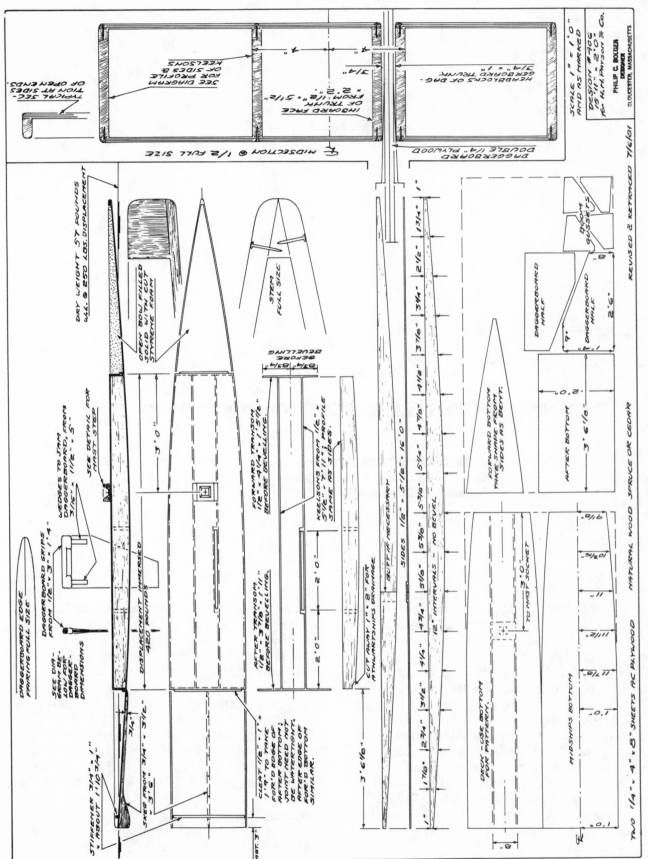

The Dynamite Sailboard, Sheet 1.

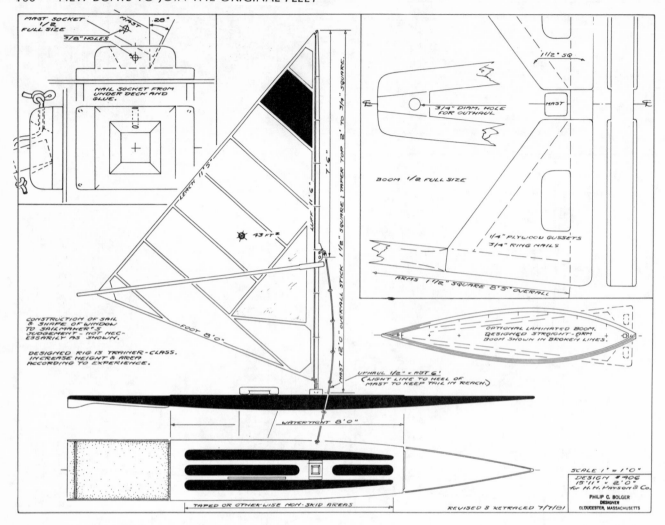

The Dynamite Sailboard, Sheet 2.

patent for what they called "Windsurfer," and shortly after, the public took their invention to its heart much as they had the Hula-hoop. That enthusiasm as yet shows no sign of diminishing.

At least, Phil and I can say that we weren't in hot pursuit of the Almighty dollar when we entered the field; what we were promoting was the economy and fun of building your own. The savings alone are considerable, a mere two hundred dollars to do it our way against the price range of six hundred to more than a thousand bucks for a store-bought version.

At this point, I will have to confess that I wasn't in command on the occasion of the Dynamite Sailboard's trials. I wanted an expert's evaluation, and I wanted to take some photographs of an expert showing what the Sailboard could do.

Dick Cadwalader took her out on Lake Chickawaukie on a warm afternoon in June 1981, under a bright sky and fluky northwest winds. I had photographer Jeff Julian with me in a June Bug, a dry-pants descendant of the Sailboard. For a while I thought the thing would never take off and go. We were running neck and neck when a gust caught the board, and she left us behind in one big hurry.

I always like watching the bow waves and the wake Phil's boats make. I well remember that on that day, the flat wake of the first Dynamite Sailboard looked as though somebody had mowed a path for her to follow.

Originally both her ends were designed to be free-flooded, with only the midsection made watertight. But during trials I discovered that the forward end needed

The Dynamite sailboard's sides, keelsons, transoms, and daggerboard trunk, all of cedar. (Jeff Julian photo)

Assembling the board. The stem — a wedge so small you can barely see it — goes in first, then the sides are bent around the forward transom to meet the stern transom. Keelsons and daggerboard trunk are in place. (Jeff Julian photo)

to be filled with Styrofoam to keep her bow up.

Dick's verdict was that she did everything a good board should do and had superior stability to boot.

Commenting on her rig, Phil says: "As noted on the plans, the sail is trainer size. We discussed increasing it, but concluded that quite properly her design was aimed at novices. I suppose that somebody who has mastered these boards will want more sail, but such a person should also know how much the *board* wants. Every so often somebody asks me how much sail area a given boat should have. In reply, I always ask how strong the wind will be."

Materials

Two sheets ¼-inch 4-by-8-foot AC exterior, marine grade, or Lauan plywood. One pound Weldwood dry powder glue or marine glue of your choice. One pound ⅞-inch number 14 bronze ring nails. Cedar, preferably, for sides, transoms, daggerboard trunk, and keelsons, sawn to the natural shape of the tree. (Pine, spruce, fir,

or mahogany is OK, but will add weight.) Clear, straight-grained 2 x 4s for wishbone boom and mast.

Construction Tips

Mark 1-foot intervals for the sides as shown; cut to shape, and cut out the keelsons (the fore-and-aft reinforcing members) using a side for a pattern. Cut limber holes in the keelsons; build the daggerboard trunk, or case, onto the keelson, then fasten forward and after transoms in place. Set the whole assembly on sawhorses and bend sides around the transoms—glue and nail the stem first, then fasten the sides to the transoms.

Cut a sheet of plywood into two 2-foot panels for the top and bottom of the midships section. Tack the bottom panel onto the hull and trace the shape around the sides. IMPORTANT: Mark around the keelsons and daggerboard trunk from inside. Take the panel off

Fitting the top panel. As with the bottom panel, trace keelson and daggerboard locations on the panel, and drill pilot holes within these guidelines. This will eliminate shotgun nailing when you tack the panel into place. (Jeff Julian photo)

Tracing the shape of the bottom bow panel. (Jeff Julian photo)

and bore pilot holes with a ⁵⁄₆₄-inch drill where marked, so you won't have to guess where to nail the panels when you fasten them for good. Before permanently nailing the bottom panel, fit and mark the top panel the same way.

If you are doubtful about your boat carpentry and the Sailboard's watertightness, bore a ¾-inch hole through the after corner of the deck for drainage, and fabricate a plug. Fill the bow section with Styrofoam, but leave the after section to free-flood.

A Dacron sail, cut and sewn to Bolger specs, is available from H. H. Payson and Company, Pleasant Beach Road, South Thomaston, Maine 04858.

Further Comments

With the goal of keeping her weight down, I chose cedar for both sides and framing. She weighed in at 57 pounds—a bit heftier than the even 50 pounds I had hoped for, but not bad for her length of 16 feet.

Building her was easy, with no tricky spots that gave me a hard time. Use plenty of glue and nails, and keep firmly in mind that it's the glue and the close fit of the bottom and deck to the sides and the forward and after transoms that is going to keep that midships box section watertight.

What concerned me most during the building process was the universal joint, or rather the lack of one, for the mast to pivot on. The joint has to be capable of ranging from mast-flat-in-the-water to a 360-degree pivoting action when she's upright. I fiddled with trying to produce a homemade device, but nothing worked. Phil came up with the solution, saying that all I had to do was to bore a hole through the foot of the mast and another through the mast step, and run a piece of shock cord through them.

This worked acceptably well; even Dick Cadwalader didn't complain about it. But I suspect that a store-bought standard universal joint might be better.

Sailing one of these boards calls for the agility and quick responses that teenagers are blessed with, along with a knack for getting them moving. To me, those who are good at it are artists in their own way. Deeply imprinted in my memory is the sight of a board sailed clear into the air from the crest of a huge comber, huge enough to please even a surfboarder. I imagine you have to log a lot of practice hours before you are ready to attempt aerobatics like that. If you're that ambitious, I recommend you sort through the considerable library of how-to books on this subject—somewhere in them

Dick Cadwalader puts the sailboard through her paces. (Jeff Julian photo)

there's something to suit the needs of every practitioner of board sailing, from beginner to postgrad.

The essentials of getting one of these craft started can be learned on dry land or on any stable platform. Just raising the sail from the horizontal to an up-and-drawing position without getting blown away is an accomplishment in itself; best master that maneuver first.

Here's how: Grab onto the uphaul—the knotted line attached directly above the forward end of the boom—and use your weight to bring the sail upright, letting it flutter. Then balance the rig, and hold the mast tilted forward with one hand while you sheet her in, as it were, with the other. Steer by raking the mast fore or aft.

In a nutshell: If you want to luff into the wind, rake your mast toward the stern; if you want to bear away from the wind, rake it forward.

Now let's proceed to a boat designed for sailors of ruddered craft who prefer a minimum of wetted surface—*their* surface, that is.

CHAPTER TWELVE

A Workhorse Called June Bug

My first impulse when I finished this 14-footer's hull was to use her, with a Dynamite Sailboard's kite rig, as a stable platform, without rudder, to perfect my free-sailing technique. It didn't work.

But a stable platform June Bug certainly is. Originally Phil designed her as a mooring tender from which to work with heavy gear such as large mushroom anchors and concrete blocks.

"I wanted her as a replacement for a used-up light dory that wasn't up to that job," he said. "I wanted the best compromise available between maximum capacity and stability on minimum overall dimensions and weight, with reasonably good performance under oars, as well as sail. I was aiming at 1,000 pounds capacity in quiet conditions, and good lines for rowing with up to a 400-pound load, and a weight, empty, of under 100 pounds."

This accounts for her plumb lines—plumb stem, plumb stern, and plumb sides. When June Bug was featured in a *Small Boat Journal* article, she sparked quite a controversy in letters to the editor about the virtues of flared sides versus vertical. I wouldn't say either side won. I'll stick in my oar by pointing out that if you load a flared-sided dory to the gunwales, she will be so stiff you can walk right around those gunwales—while you couldn't even venture near them if she is lightly loaded. At the same time the heavy load gives her stability, it makes her vulnerable to filling. In a boat with vertical sides, you can stand right alongside her gunwales and work overboard from there. She has very high initial stability but lacks the reserve buoyancy of the flared-sided model, and if you push her too far, she will dump you.

On balance, from my point of view, I can get just as wet and just as drowned in one as I can in the other.

In considering the question of boat shape and the aesthetics of various types of hulls, I keep thinking back to the first round-bottomed, carvel-planked lobsterboat I ever designed and built. I wanted some tumblehome around the stern section, but I overbent the tops of her timbers so much that when I took the molds out she had tumblehome sides from stem to transom. With her hollow waterline forward, she strongly resembled a cigar, but a good workboat she was. Later on I sold her to a math teacher at Rockland High School, who used her for lobster fishing and patched her and patched her until there was nothing left to patch, claiming she was the best workboat he was ever in. Somewhere through the years I threw away the half-model I built her from, and now I wish I'd kept it.

The June Bug design caught the eye of Jeff Julian, a

104

June Bug, Sheet 1.

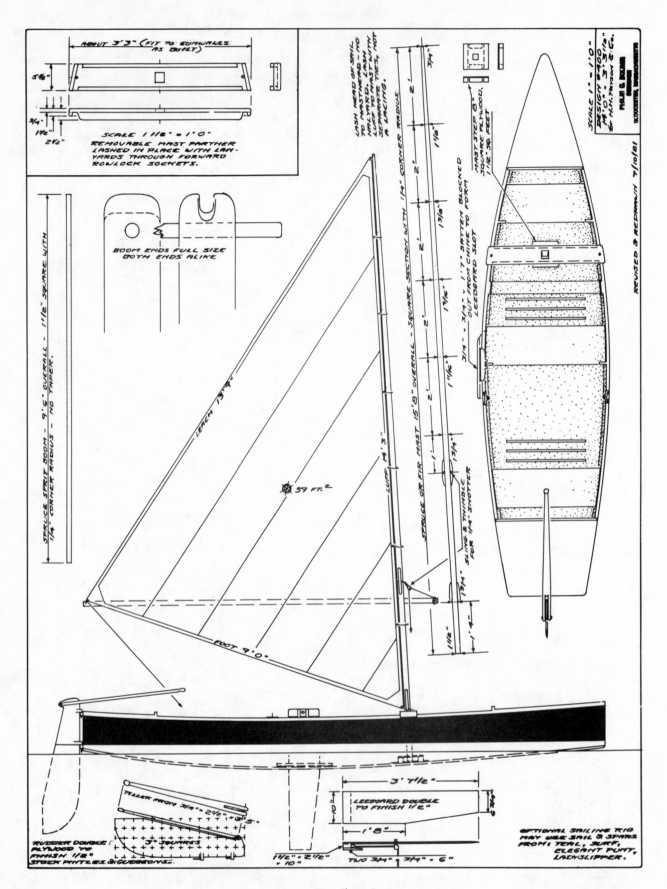

June Bug, Sheet 2.

Note the wild grain of the yellow pine plywood I used in June Bug's sides. This plywood is heavier than the more common fir variety. (Jeff Julian photo)

boatman, photographer, and friend, and he and I built the prototype together for him and his wife Cathie. That was in June 1982, which accounts for half of her name.

She carries the same sprit rig I first met up with in the original fleet of Instant Boats, but the rig differs from the original in one detail. Her sprit rides parallel to the water instead of being cocked up at the after end. To my mind, this offers a mechanical advantage in that it makes it easier to set the clew up tight.

June Bug goes together easily enough, with no bothersome bugs to trip you up.

Materials

• Four sheets ¼-inch 4-by-8-foot AC exterior or marine grade plywood. Three 16-foot 2 x 4s for chine logs, gunwales, frames, etc. Pine, spruce, fir, or mahogany boards for mast partner, side frames, and wherever stock from 2 x 4s won't work.
• Two pounds Weldwood dry powder glue or marine glue of your choice. Two pounds each, ¾-inch and ⅞-

inch bronze ring nails. One pound smooth number 14- and number 18-wire copper nails. One gallon Interlux number 1026 clear wood sealer. Two quarts each, undercoater and finish.
• Thirty-five feet 3-inch fiberglass tape. One quart resin, with hardener.
• One set ½-inch gudgeons and pintles (Wilcox, Crittenden numbers 4627 and 4601, respectively). Two pair oarlocks and two pair side plates (Wilcox, Crittenden numbers 4477 and 4482, respectively). One 2-inch cleat for luff line, or make from wood as shown on sail plan. One ¼-inch thimble for snotter.

Layout and Assembly

For sides, lay two sheets of plywood on the floor, butted end-to-end and tacked down to prevent movement. Mark off as shown at 1-foot intervals (with one 3-inch interval at the bow), drawing lines across the entire width of the sheets. Measure in from the bottom edge to the given dimensions, drive wire brads, and spring a batten along the brads to draw the sheer and chine profiles.

Glue and fasten a butt strap to the side panel, using copper nails driven through into the floor. Pry up the edge of the plywood and wedge scrap under the side area to clear it for sawing without disturbing the rest of the layout. Cut the side panel with a Skilsaw, and bend nail points over. With the side panel flipped to make a mirror-image pattern, lay it on the remaining surface of the butted plywood sheets, scribe around it, and repeat the butt-strap procedure. Seat heights are given on frame molds 1 and 2, and the stern-seat height can be scaled from the plan profile. With the sides laid flat on the floor, align and mark the locations of all three seats (forward edge of stern seat is 2 feet 8 inches from aft edge of frame mold 2).

Draw the frame molds full size to the dimensions indicated, and assemble as drawn. Frame 1 requires a side bevel of 11 degrees and a bottom bevel of 3½ degrees. Frame 2 is not beveled.

Cut limber holes. For chine-log notches, make only horizontal cuts, leaving corners on until the frame molds are fastened to the sides; then cut out corners. The transom requires a side bevel of 11 degrees and a bottom bevel of 10½ degrees. There is no need for chine-log notches in the transom if a good chine-log end fit can be achieved.

Stand sides upside down on the floor or on sawhorses. Glue and fasten frame mold 2, pull sides together at bow and stern, install frame mold 1, the stem, and the transom, and install chine logs. (If the

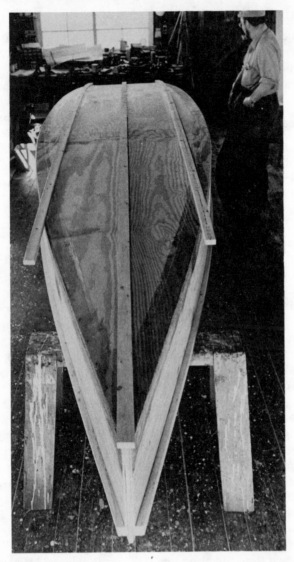

Left: *The bottom panel is on. As with all the Instant Boats, tape the chines before fastening the skids.* **Right:** *Bow and seat areas are filled with Styrofoam, and seat tops, foredeck, and foot brace battens are installed. (Jeff Julian photo)*

side panels won't hold their curve over the long run between frame mold 2 and the transom, install the stern-seat framing temporarily for additional bracing.) Using the assembly, establish the true shape of the forward and after bottom sections and cut. Place back on. When satisfied with the fit, slip the butt strap under the bottom, scribe its ends for a slack fit to the chine logs, and glue and fasten the butt strap right on the spot. Remove the bottom assembly, spread glue on the chine logs and frames liberally, replace the bottom, and fasten.

The bottom skids go on after the chines have been glass taped. Mark their locations and bore staggered

pilot holes for nails from the outside. Glue the skids and drive nails from the inside.

Turn the boat right side up and complete the interior.

A Dacron sail, cut and sewn to Bolger specs, is available from H. H. Payson and Company.

Further Comments

I've had phone calls from a couple of builders about the rigging of the removable mast partner. As you see on the plan, it rests right across the oarlock side plates in

What June Bug lacks in looks, she makes up for in performance. (Jeff Julian photo)

the forward rowing position. If two oarsmen are rowing, or if for any reason you want to row solo from the forward position, you have to unstep the mast and remove the partner.

Check out the little drawing in the upper left-hand corner of the sail-plan sheet. As the end-on view shows, there are little ears on the partner, port and starboard, which hook over the gunwales. The top view, which includes the hole for the mast, indicates two small holes bored port and starboard. These are bored to receive short lanyards led down through the oarlock side plate sockets. The ends of the lanyards are knotted underneath the mast partner to hold it securely in place.

Jeff and I took our time building her, partly because he was making a series of photographs of the project and partly because he wanted to learn the ins and outs of building. Working at that leisurely pace we completed June Bug's hull in one week and spent another two days on her sailing rig components.

We went about 50 pounds over the 100 Phil designed her for, primarily because we decided to use yellow pine plywood. Yellow pine is about twice as heavy as fir, but you're not much aware of the difference, handling one sheet at a time. You're surprised only when you've finished the whole thing.

June Bug proved her stability during her sailing and rowing trials, and I never felt nervous about her plumb sides. She carries a load well and has no vices, in my experience.

CHAPTER THIRTEEN

The Handy 10½-Foot Pointy Skiff

The Pointy Skiff was designed with the working fisherman in mind, but she serves the pleasure-seeking boater just as well. Loaded with a couple of tubs of bait, spare gas, two grown men, and the usual mishmash thrown in, her ample freeboard and her 4-foot 2-inch beam ensure safe passage from dock to mother ship even in a moderately steep chop. Or you can substitute the average family picnic for the above load and head for a nearby island.

I planned to use her for fishing myself, but I dropped out of lobstering just about then and shelved the plans until I got my activities a little better organized. I gave a set to the Region Eight Vocational School in Rockland, but I had completely forgotten about that until one day I saw their prototype sitting on a fisherman's float.

She was built twice as heavy as needed, starting with a ⅞-inch crossplanked bottom instead of the ⅜-inch plywood called for and proceeding with heftier seats, extra framing—the works. But she looked as she was supposed to. Ironically, it turned out she had been bought by my brother-in-law, who has never had a kind word for anything Phil Bolger designed. When he said, "It's the best skiff I ever owned," weight and all, I decided not to press the matter.

The Pointy Skiff rows well with 6- to 6½-foot oars, and a 2 or 3 h.p. outboard drives her easily. More than

that would be wasted; it wouldn't make her go much faster and would only add more weight and bother.

If you object to small motors because they don't have any reverse, just remember that you can fill that void by turning them around 180 degrees. When you do, slow the motor down to idle, and don't hesitate once you start swiveling it around. Ned Grade, a New York English teacher and the owner-builder of the 7-foot 9-inch Elegant Punt included in my first book, *Instant Boats*, was teaching his young son how to do this with the mini-motor he had hung on her transom. He got as far as "This is how to..." when they found themselves up to their necks in water. He had paused just long enough at 90 degrees hard over to flip her in one quick motion, furnishing a prime example of the old saw about he who hesitates.

Let's collect the makings and get one of these Pointy Skiffs in the water.

Materials

• Two sheets ¼-inch 4-by-8-foot AC exterior plywood. One sheet ⅜-inch 4-by-8-foot AC exterior 4-ply plywood for bottom. (If you can't get 4-ply, use ½-inch AC exterior 5-ply or, alternatively, use two sheets of ¼-

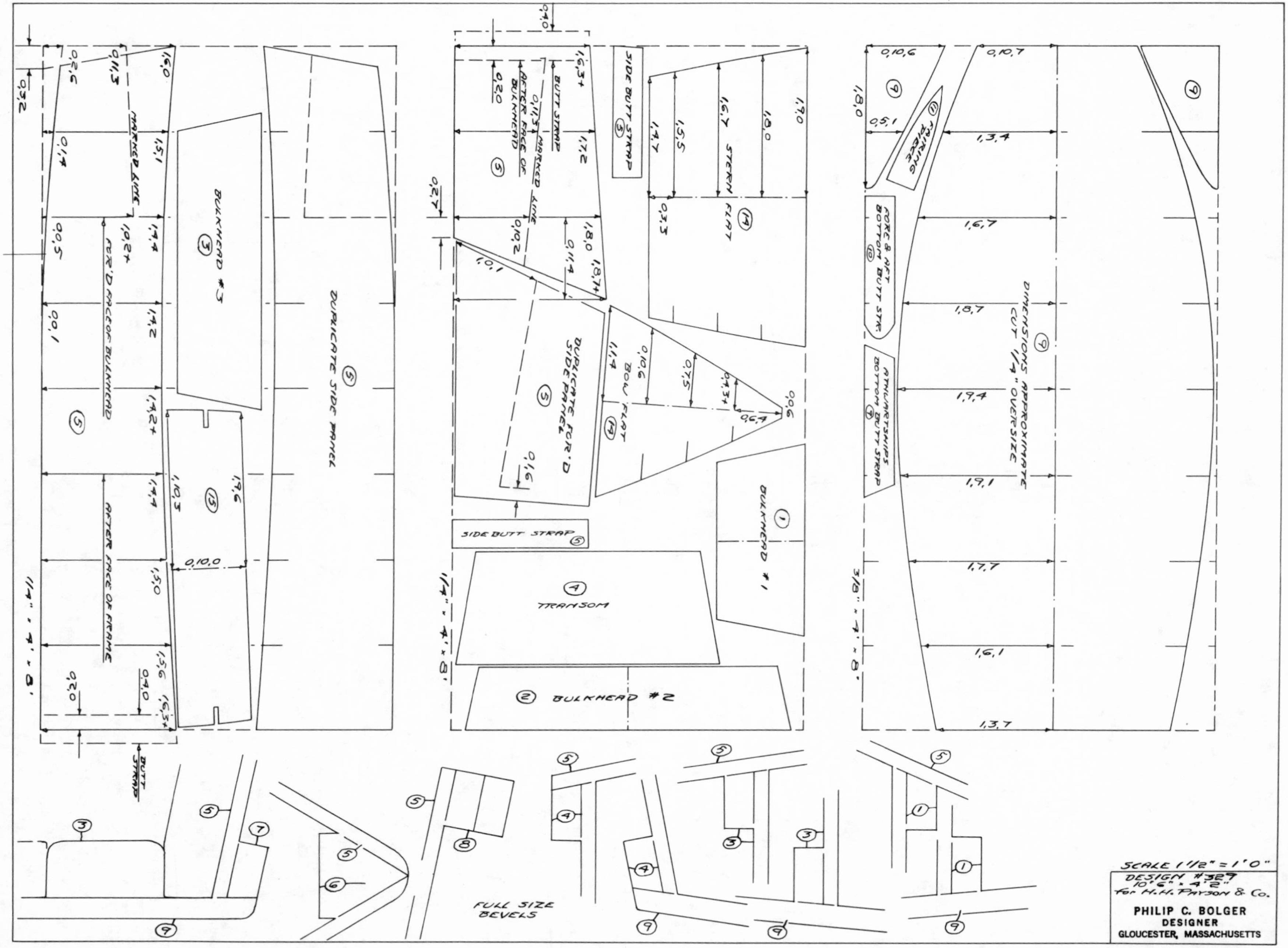

SCALE 1/12" = 1' 0"
DESIGN #387
10' 6" × 4' 2"
FOR H.H. PAYSON & Co.
PHILIP C. BOLGER
DESIGNER
GLOUCESTER, MASSACHUSETTS

⑨

DIMENSIONS APPROXIMATE
CUT 1/4" OVERSIZE
⑨

0,0,7 1,3,4 1,6,7 1,8,7 1,9,4 1,9,1 1,7,7 1,6,1 1,3,7

⑪ FAIRING PIECE

0,10,0 ⑨ 1,5,0

FORE & AFT BOTTOM BUTT STR. ⑩

ATHWARTSHIPS BOTTOM BUTT STRAP ⑦

1,8,0

3/8" × 4' × 8'

⑤ ⑪
⑪
⑨

③
⑦

1,9,0
1,8,0
⑭ STERN FLAT
1,6,7
1,5,5
1,4,7 0,3,3

SIDE BUTT STRAP ③

0,0,6
0,4,3+
0,7,5
0,10,6
BOW FLAT
1,1,4 ⑭

①
BULKHEAD #1

⑤
⑤
④

1,6,3+ 1,7,2 1,8,0 1,8,7+
0,11,4
BUTT STRAP
MARKED LINE
0,11,5
AFTER FACE OF BULKHEAD 0,10,2
0,2,0 ⑤
0,4,0
0,2,7

DUPLICATE FOR'D SIDE PANEL
⑤
0,1,6
SIDE BUTT STRAP ⑤

④ TRANSOM

② BULKHEAD #2

⑤
⑤
⑤ ⑥
⑦
⑤
⑦

FULL SIZE BEVELS

⑧

1/4" × 4' × 8'

⑤
DUPLICATE SIDE PANEL

BULKHEAD #3
③

1,9,6
⑮
0,10,0

1,10,3

1,6,0 1,5,1 1,4,4 1,4,2 1,4,2+ 1,4,4 1,5,0 1,5,6 1,6,3+
MARKED LINE 0,4,0
0,11,3 1,0,2+ BUTT STRAP
FOR'D FACE OF BULKHEAD AFTER FACE OF FRAME ③
0,2,6 0,1,4 0,0,5 0,0,1 ⑤ 0,2,0
0,3,2

1/4" × 4' × 8'

Pointy Skiff, Sheet 1.

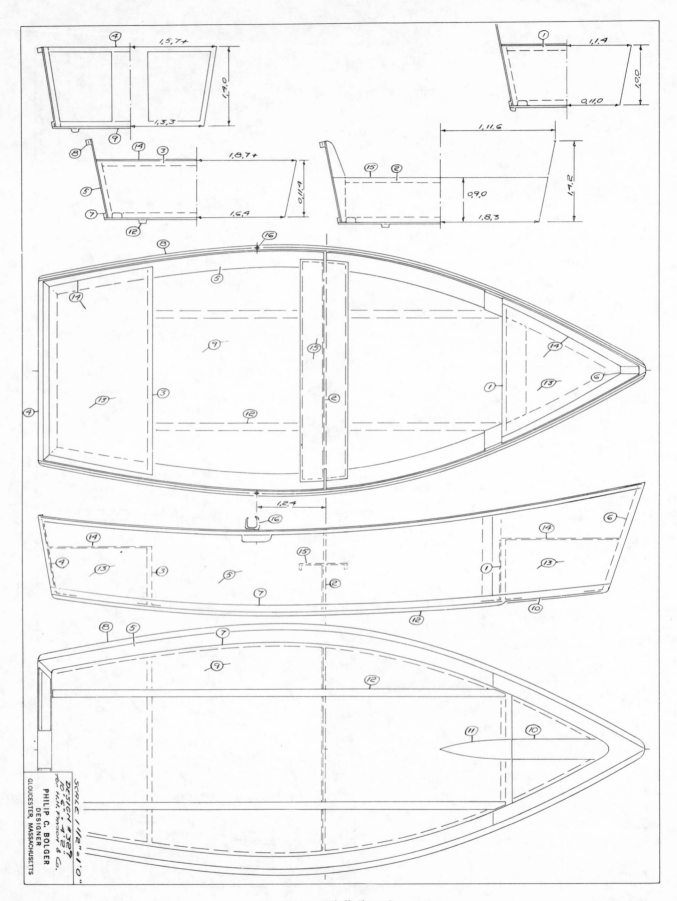

Pointy Skiff, Sheet 2.

KEY

1. First bulkhead ¼'' plywood; plywood faces aft; ½'' or ¾'' x 1'' fastening frame all around; bevel after edges ⁷⁄₁₆'' in 1'' to make a sharp after edge to jam against forward edge of side butt straps when bending sides around.

2. Second bulkhead the same, except that side frames are from ½'' or ¾'' x 2½'' x about 1'5'' to come up to gunwale.

3. Third bulkhead like first; see drawing for dimensions; note that in all three bulkheads the fastening frame just stops clear of the limber holes each side.

4. Transom same as bulkheads except no limber holes; note that frame is on the outside; outboard motor board ¾'' x 7½'' or more wide optional.

5. Sides ¼'' plywood cut out to diagram and assembled on 4''-wide butt straps as shown; get straps accurately centered on the butt as they locate #1 bulkhead. Make sure the two sides are right- and left-handed as to butt straps and marks for bulkheads and end flats. (Secure sides to #2 bulkhead frame and bring ends in around bulkheads to stem and transom; better take them in a little at a time, alternately bow and stern, with a rope loop to hold each gain on the bend while you take in the other end some more. Glue and nail permanently, making sure of no holidays in the glue at stem and transom.)

6. Stem beveled to full-size section given, from 1½'' square, secured to one (either) side plank.

7. Chine logs from ⅝'' x 1'', glued, clamped, and nailed to assembled sides.

8. Gunwale clamps double ½'' x 1'' (i.e., to finish 1'' square).

9. Bottom ⅜'' plywood, cut out to fit assembled sides; note that the athwartships butt strap is offset ahead to clear #1 bulkhead.

10. Fore-and-aft bottom butt strap on the outside.

11. Fairing piece.

12. Bottom shoes ¾'' x 1½'', sprung on and nailed from inside; might be smart to use screws and not glue them, so they can be replaced when worn. They ought not to be left off, or moved much, as they're meant to serve as supporting slings for the bottom, to make it harder to stamp her open at the chine.

13. Foam buoyancy sawn up and packed, or expanded in place. With this foam all in place, the boat can be rowed full of water, and bailed out when swamped even if the water is not quite smooth.

14. End flats ¼'' plywood, with ½'' x 1'' cleats on hull sides for support; if motor is likely, fasten stern flat securely to about 1½'' square cleat all across the inside of the transom. Cut end flats ½'' larger all around than shown to allow for scribe fit.

15. Rowing thwart ¼'' plywood, to diagram after checking actual space; rest on top of bulkhead with ½'' x 1'' (or more) stiffener each edge plus cleats on hull sides.

16. Rowlock sockets conventional ½''; location shown is for Bolger rowlocks or for thole pins or brackets; if center-shank rowlocks are used place about an inch farther aft.

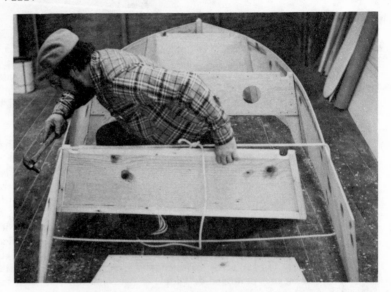

With the side panels upside down on the floor, they are fastened to the forward and midframe molds and to the stem, then to the after frame mold, and finally to the transom.

inch glued together; don't use ⅜-inch marine grade—it costs an arm and a leg.) Three or four clear 12-foot 2 x 4s to make up gunwales, chine logs, drag strips or skids, and framing.

● One pound each, ¾-inch, 1-inch, and 1⅛-inch number 13 bronze anchor nails. One-half pound, 1-inch number 13 or number 14 smooth-wire copper nails. One box, 1-inch number 9 brass or bronze screws. Two pounds Weldwood dry powder glue or a marine glue of your choice.

● One pint epoxy resin with hardener. Twenty-five feet of 3-inch fiberglass tape. Two quarts each, plywood primer and finish paint.

● One set Wilcox, Crittenden oarlocks and side plates.

Layout and Assembly

When laying off the parts for assembly, note that the numbers 1 through 16 on the drawings are keyed to the numbered list of the parts accompanying the plans, and not to the order of assembly.

My building procedure varies somewhat from the layout of the parts' patterns shown by Bolger on the plans. Bolger's plans indicate that the forward and after sections of the side panels would be traced on separate plywood sheets, cut out separately, and then butted together. This procedure would use the plywood most efficiently but at an increased expenditure of time. Instead, butt two sheets of plywood together first. Mark both long edges of the plywood sheets at 1-foot intervals and draw lines across with a straightedge.

Bending the nail points over on the forward-bottom panel's internal butt strap.

Note that the interval at the extreme bow end of the side panels is 0-11-4, or 11½ inches, instead of the 12 inches used elsewhere.

Next, mark off on the lines, from the plywood edges, the measurements to the chine and sheer of each side panel. Working from nails or brads driven in halfway on the marks, sweep the chine and sheer curves with a batten long enough to continue a fair curve beyond the

A fine fisherman's skiff for oar or small motor.

ends of these shapes. Mark the side panels for frame mold and seat-frame locations. Buttstrap the forward-side panels to the longer after-side panels, gluing and fastening with copper nails. Cut the sides out, and bend the nails over where they protrude.

The bottom is laid out from two pieces—a large one running from the transom, and a smaller one at the forward end consisting of a small triangle that extends the bottom to the stem. Don't butt the pieces together until assembly is underway.

The Pointy Skiff goes together in the same fashion as most of the plywood-paneled Instant Boats: sides placed bottom up and nailed to frame molds, stem, and transom.

Next the chine logs go on, followed by the bottom. Rather than cut out the bottom to the dimensions on the plan, plop the plywood sheet on the sides and mark around underneath to get an exact fit. Butt the triangular forward-bottom panel internally and also externally, where the butt strap will also serve to absorb beaching wear; cut the after end of the butt strap to a streamlined shape, or add a small tailpiece with this shape to the butt itself. Next, glue and fasten the drag

strips to the bottom. These strips are ¾ inch by 1½ inches in cross section. Prebore pilot holes to accept the nails, apply glue, spring the strips into place, and fasten, driving the nails from the inside.

(**Note:** *Be sure to fasten the drag strips before you finish out the interior. Otherwise, you won't be able to drive the nails from the inside.*)

Install the forward and after flats (seat tops). Paint the inside of the resulting cavities and fill them with Styrofoam for flotation. I recommend installing cleats to raise the Styrofoam clear of the bottom, so it won't absorb spilled gas or oil.

Further Comments

The oarlock locations indicated on the plans are for Bolger-type oarlocks, or tholepins. If you use the standard center-shank oarlocks specified in the list of materials, move them aft about one inch. The location of the rowing thwart, which rests on top of the number 2 bulkhead and on cleats on the hull sides, is supposed to be right for bracing your feet against the face of the number 3 bulkhead. I recommend setting a few cleats, say ¾ inch by 1½ inches by 6 inches, at distances suitable to accommodate the various leg lengths of male, female, and juvenile rowers. Any boat rows very hard and is not really safe, either, if the rower's feet slide. For convenient oar storage, I cut holes in the number 2 bulkhead to receive them.

If frequent use of a motor is likely, I would fasten a ¾-by-7½-inch motor board to the transom.

CHAPTER FOURTEEN

The Pedal-Driven Sidewheeler

She was named Madeline and came about her name quite naturally from the old song "Paddlin' Madeline Home." This is what her owner shot back at me when I asked what he was going to call her.

I suppose I live quite a sheltered life tucked way up here in my corner of the country, for when Peter Hoe Burling, an attorney in Claremont, New Hampshire (way inland) called two winters ago wanting to know if I would build him a pedal boat, I had never heard of one.

Phone calls in the middle of the winter get a warm welcome from me when they have to do with boatbuilding; they always jingle me up a little with thoughts of spring and a summer spent on the water. After surviving the doldrums of Christmas and the New Year, I look forward to calls like that as much as I look forward to the first robin.

Peter developed his yen for a pedal boat while vacationing in the Caribbean and watching a fellow trying to operate a spectacularly unsuccessful one. Immediately on his return he commissioned Phil to design him a two-seater to match his palm-tree dream, and as soon as he got his hands on the plans he rang my number. Phil had told him that it was a good idea to get plans to me well in advance, since he knows that I like to take a lot of time brooding over new designs—

especially in the early stages, and you couldn't call these finished plans; a lot of measurements for angles of cuts were still missing.

Not that the hull itself posed any problem. The straight-cut sides, for example, are as simple as Windsprint's—as easy as you can get. But there were no measurements for the slots in the frame molds for the fore-and-aft beams of the paddle box to fit in. So if you decide to build this one, plan on giving your scale rule plenty of use. The facts are there, but even in the revised plans, you will have to dig some of them out with that rule. Keep it handy.

To give another example: To find the tapers on the after ends of the fore-and-aft beams and the intermediate beams and the forward ends of the paddle beams, project a straight line across their tops and measure the angle from that line.

Again, slight angles like the one on top of the after end of the fore-and-aft beam (showing the seat rest) are easy to miss, viewed in profile, so hold the plans edgewise at eyeball level and look along the top of the beam. Now that slight angle jumps right out at you, but you might have missed it just looking at it straight on in profile.

Keep in mind that the whole paddle assembly calls for relatively close tolerances. You have to maintain

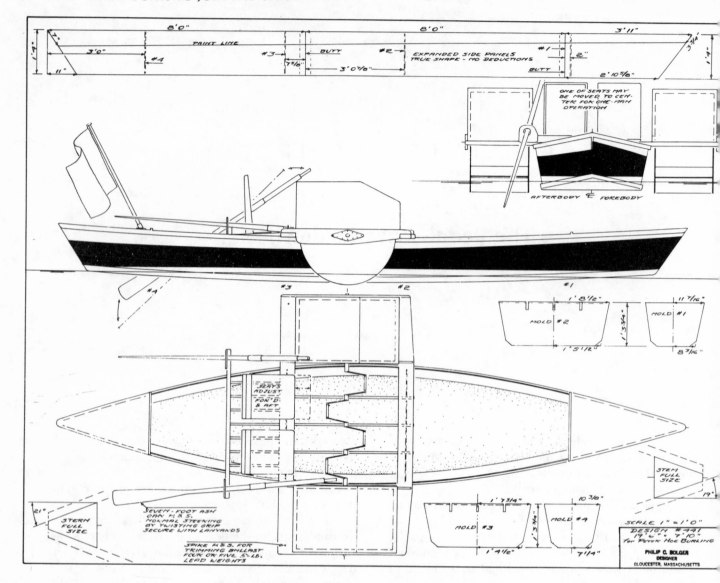

Pedal-Driven Sidewheeler, Sheet 1.

about quarter-inch clearances between the gunwales and the inboard sides of the paddle boxes; to ensure that, I marked the location of the boxes right on the two 2 x 6 transverse beams as a reference and a reminder that the quarter-inch clearance was not to be violated.

Unless you are an experienced worker in metal, I suggest you do as I did and subcontract the manufacture of the pedal shaft. I turned this job over to Richard Ilvonen, a first-rate welder in nearby Owls Head. He in turn subcontracted the cutting and shaping of the stainless steel parts to a metal fabricating firm.

It seemed wise to give this part of the construction a

head start as I foresaw no difficulties in readying the boat for the installation. I gave Richard a set of plans early in the game, before I had even started the hull. When the hull was done and the paddle assembly ready, there was still no shaft. I'll spare you the details, but the reasons for the delay, listed by the fabricator, ranged from vacation time to bad backs. When the pieces were finally delivered, most were satisfactory but a few were not, and getting everything welded together gave Richard a very hard time.

The moral of this is, track down the best machine shop you can find that's close enough that you can check progress daily. All the delays, cutting, recutting,

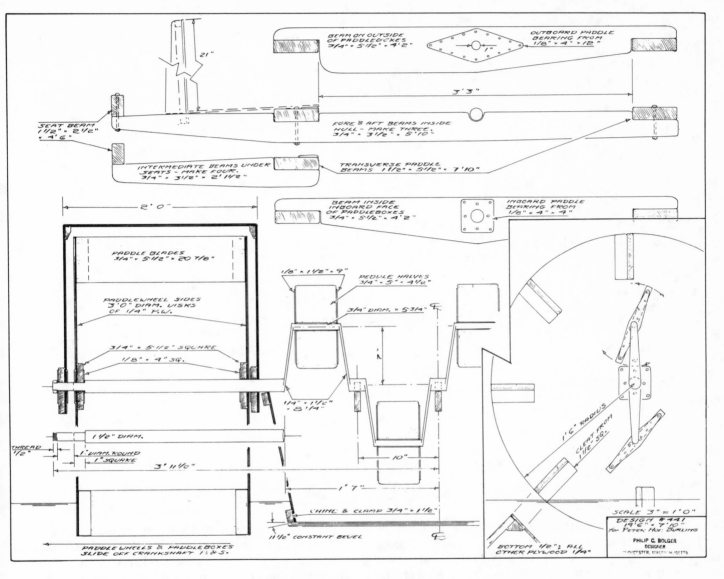

Pedal-Driven Sidewheeler, Sheet 2.

and fiddling, including the price of the stainless steel itself, brought the cost of the shaft and its components to $800. With all this, it took about 182 hours to build her, of which only about 36 hours were devoted to the hull. Materials, excluding the pedal shaft, cost $376. Constructing the Pedal-Driven Sidewheeler is not an inexpensive proposition, but with a decent machine shop, it certainly need not approach the cost of Madeline.

In the original plan, the Pedal Boat's steering system consisted of two 7-foot ash oars mounted on the seat beam port and starboard, which works well enough as long as both operators agree on the course. But it was a little like having a car with two steering wheels, each working independently of the other.

From the start, Peter obviously had some misgivings about this rig, because he had me install gudgeons on her stern post on which to hang the rudder he had Phil design for him after our trials. This is the rudder shown in the drawing, but we used only one yoke arm, shortened to a length of 1 foot and mounted horizontally instead of cocked as drawn. Peter also rejected the tiller-rope system, so we used a rigid pole—a closet pole, in fact—with an eye driven into one end linked to an eye on the yoke arm to form a serviceable, if slightly crude, universal joint. The shortened yoke arm, in addition to keeping the rig farther inboard, allowed straighter in-line control of steering.

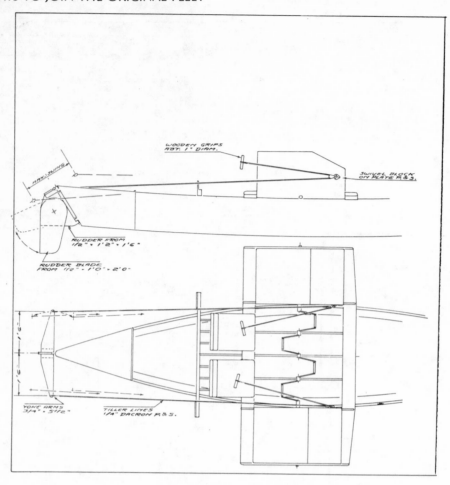

Pedal-Driven Sidewheeler, Sheet 3.

I must admit that all during the building of Madeline I was a bit skeptical, thinking she was going to be awkward to pedal and very tiring and that the moment you stopped pedaling, unlike a bicycle, she would simply come to a halt. Phil hadn't been very reassuring, saying that he offered no guarantee this boat would work. If anyone else had said that, I probably would have said "You're right," and dropped the whole project. But with my experiences building his 31-foot Folding Schooner, the bow-steering Query, and Tortoise with her mast stuck way forward against her starboard side, among other unconventional Bolger designs that were all different from anything I'd ever seen or heard of before and all of which surprised me, I decided this one, too, deserved a try.

I'm glad I did, for the first time we put her in the water one July evening, her prospective owner and I pedaled away any negative feelings I'd had about the craft. Pedaling her was easy, not the least bit awkward but a nice pleasant exercise you could keep up for quite

some time; Phil had gotten the amount of paddle dip and foot pedal leverage exactly right. I liked the chuffing sound of the paddle wheels, a rhythmic accompaniment that reminded me of an old steam train getting up speed. The speed surprised me, too. Oh, she was no race horse, and she definitely preferred quiet water, but the two of us got her up to a steady seven knots with no strain.

Materials

● Five sheets ¼-inch 4-by-8-foot AC exterior or marine grade plywood for sides, paddle boxes, paddle wheels, and frame molds. Two sheets ½-inch 4-by-8-foot AC exterior or marine grade plywood for bottom. One sheet ¾-inch 4-by-8-foot plywood, same grade, for paddle wheel blades. Three 1½-inch-by-6-inch 8-foot planks for transverse paddle beams, seat beams, and miscellaneous framing. Two 16-foot 2 x 4s—spruce, fir, pine, or mahogany—for the gunwales and chine logs.

- One small box, 1-inch number 10 flathead bronze screws for inboard paddle bearings. One small box, ⅞-inch number 12 roundhead bronze screws for outboard paddle bearings. Twenty-one 4½-inch-by-¼-inch bronze carriage bolts. One pound 1¼-inch bronze anchor nails. One pound 1-inch smooth-wire copper nails. One pound Weldwood dry powder glue or epoxy or marine glue of your choice.
- Fifty feet of 3-inch fiberglass tape for chines, stem, and stern post and for taping in frame molds if desired. One quart resin with hardener. One quart epoxy or polyester resin for sealer. One gallon undercoater paint. Two quarts finish.

Layout and Assembly

Butt three sheets of ¼-inch plywood end-to-end; lay out hull sides (mirror images), and mark frame mold locations. Glue and fasten butt straps with copper nails, and clinch their points over. Cut out sides and place bottom up on floor or sawhorses. Cut frame molds 1 through 4. After cutting the notches for the fore-and-aft beams in frame molds 2 and 3, tack in the frame molds for glass taping later in this order: 2, 3, 1, 4. Fasten the sides to the stem and the stern post. Cut the chine logs, bevel 11½ degrees, and fasten them from inside. Check the chine logs for a flat fit to the bottom, and mark centerlines on both sides of the after-bottom plywood sheet.

Tack the sheet to the stern post and align the centerline with the centerlines on frame molds 3 and 4. Trace around sides for the shape of the after bottom, remove the sheet, and cut out the after-bottom panel. Replace the panel on the hull, slip a 6-inch-wide butt strap in place under its forward edge, fit the butt strap, fasten it to the panel, and then glue and fasten the bottom on for good. Butt the middle-bottom sheet to the after-bottom panel, repeat the fitting procedure, and fasten to the butt strap already in place. One more tab forward completes the bottom. Round off the edges and glass-tape the chines, stem, and stern post.

Turn the hull right side up and install gunwales. Seal and paint the interior. Fasten a block to the underside of the afterdeck to catch screws for the flagstaff socket before fastening the deck in place.

Paddle Beams

Cut three fore-and-aft beams, ¾ inch by 3½ inches by 5 feet 10 inches. Use your scale rule in addition to the measurements specified on the pl... shapes, and cut the tapers. These bea... notches in frame molds 2 and 3. (Cut the notch... you install the frame molds.)

Fasten the transverse paddle beams (1½ inches by 5½ inches by 7 feet 10 inches) with ¼-inch bronze carriage bolts. Square the assembly by measuring diagonally across the corners of the transverse beams. Measure inboard from the beam ends to establish the clearance between the sides of the paddle boxes and the gunwales (only about ¼ inch). Mark it well; ensure that the paddle boxes will fit between these marks and the ends of the beams. Resist the temptation to make the paddle blades longer or to make any change that would affect the width of the paddle boxes as shown in plan view.

Cut the intermediate beams and bolt them to the seat beam and after transverse beam. Make the seat bottoms from ½-inch plywood. The backrests are made from ¼-inch plywood and are raked 7 degrees aft of the perpendicular from the seats, not square to the seats as shown.

Make the four paddle-box beams to locate inside and outside each box. Mark and bore for the pedal shaft. Cut the sides of the paddle boxes and bore for the shaft. Clamp the sides to the beams, but don't fasten the sides to the beams permanently yet.

Shaft and Wheels

The shaft should be 1 inch longer overall than shown to make allowance for standard-sized nuts and any slight adjustments. Nuts must be fastened to the shaft with cotter pins. I repeat, pick a good machine shop for this job, one close by so you can keep track of progress; it will pay off in savings of time and money.

In laying out the paddle wheels, two nails driven through a stick will serve adequately as a compass. Mark the locations of the blades, but don't install them yet. Bore holes for the pedal shaft in each paddlewheel side. Unclamp the paddle-box sides (note the distinction between these and the paddlewheel sides) from the beams.

On each side of the boat, slide the inboard beam and its bearing onto the shaft; repeat with the inboard paddlewheel side, its shaft block (unlabeled but dimensioned ¾-inch-by-5½-inches square on the plan), and its bearing; repeat with the outboard bearing, shaft block, paddlewheel side, and outside bearing; and finish with the outboard beam and its bearing. With the parts correctly aligned on the shaft, glue and fasten the

Installing inboard and outboard paddlewheel bearings.

Checking shaft alignment. Pedal halves not yet installed on cranks.

Installing outboard paddle beam bearing. When it is determined that both wheels are turning in sync and without binding, the paddle box ends and tops will be closed in.

paddlewheel-side bearings and shaft blocks to their respective members. Fastening these crucial parts together on the shaft is the most certain way to avoid misalignment. Now slide the wheels off the shaft, glue and fasten the paddle beams to the paddle-box sides, and install the beam bearings. Reassemble all the parts on the shaft and frame the paddle box to close in its top and ends.

Make the pedal halves from boards, not plywood.

Steering Rig and Trim

Choose from the alternative steering systems already described. The prototype's owner chose a rudder with a 1-foot arm and rigid pole linkage for push-pull steering and had good results.

The paddle assembly can be adjusted forward as much as 10 inches by sliding it along the gunwales. A bag or other container of weights, hung outboard from the after transverse paddle beam, can be used to equalize variations in trim required by the differing weights of the passengers.

Paddlin' Madeline on the Wessaweskeag River, with Peter Burling and myself providing power. Peter's heavier than I am, so there's a bag of rocks hanging outboard on my side to improve balance.

The decision to build or not to build the Pedal-Driven Sidewheeler, as with any craft under consideration, must be based on careful analysis of on-the-water needs and desires—only more so. Do you want to go out in strong winds and choppy waters? If so, look elsewhere. But if you have a yen for something different, as my client did, and have a range of weather to choose from that is on the easy side, a pedal boat can be the source of pleasant exercise and a novel way to go.

CHAPTER FIFTEEN

The 23½-Foot Light Schooner

At the time of writing, I have yet to build this craft. I include it here because Phil Bolger tells me that several have already been built to his plans and have proved themselves both as suitable projects for the home builder and as satisfyingly able sailors. "No bugs, no snags, no vices," he says.

I have built three of the 31-foot Folding Schooners featured in *Instant Boats*, and on studying these plans, I can see that this smaller nonfolding schooner will offer no problems to the backyard builder. So, with Phil's certification and blessing, I welcomed her as a worthy addition to the fleet of Instant Boats. His own name for her is simply "Scooner," without the usual "h." Here's more of what he has to say about her.

Bob Wainwright commissioned this design, and it incorporates a number of his ideas. I proposed a simpler version, with jibheaded sails and no deck—but he insisted, and I've since concluded he was right. He wanted speed, enough speed to spice up the quaintness of the rig.

So I piled on sail, 266 square feet counting the main staysail. The traditional schooner rig is about the best for carrying lots of area without going high. Reaching in a fresh breeze and not too much sea, with four or five people on the rail to hold her up, she can pass almost anything short of a C-cat. I flinch at the phrase 'planing hull,' because I think it's misused and overused. Almost

anything will plane if there's power enough, but it's true that this little schooner will skitter like a bobsled.

In stronger winds, or with a light crew, she can shorten down, like my other small schooners, to full foresail and reefed mainsail, still perfectly balanced. The geometrical center of sail area (I don't say "center of effort," because that implies a much better knowledge of thrust vectors than I or anybody has) is abaft the nominal center of lateral plane. This puts some of the side thrust on the rudder, which, being powerful and far aft, carries it with very little angle and helps lift her to windward.

The two cockpits are long enough to sleep in, supposedly with the sails for tents, although I didn't get around to examining in detail just how that would be arranged. The motor and fuel are cut off from the rest so there won't be spilled outboard mix underfoot. I see that I also didn't show the very necessary cover for the aperture of the motor well. Probably I didn't see any specially neat way to fit it and hoped the builder would come up with a better idea than any of mine. This is a well-established designer's gambit and sometimes works.

I have extracted these comments, with permission, from Bolger's recent book, *Thirty-Odd Boats*, published by International Marine Publishing Company.

Scooner, Sheet 1.

CONSTRUCTION & PERFORMANCE REPORTED ALL SATISFACTORY AFTER TWO SEASONS TRIAL. OCTOBER 18, 1982

HULL FROM BELOW

ABOUT 6" STAGGER IN BOTTOM BUTTS

EXPANDED SIDES - TRUE SHAPE - NO DEDUCTIONS

MARK FOR BULKHEAD

BUTT

MARKS FOR BULKHEADS

BUTT

MARK FOR BULKHEAD

8'0"

8'0"

3'1⅝"

3'11¾"

2'0"

2'0¼"

1'6"

1'9½"

2¼"

1'8¾"

1'7½"

1'12"

12" 12" 12" 12" 12" 12"
1'9½" 1'9" 1'8⅝" 1'9⅜" 1'8¼" 1'8¼"
4⅛" 3¾" 2⅝" 1⅜" 1⅛" ¾" 1"
5⁷⁄₁₆"
5"
3¾"

TILLER FROM 1½" - 2½"

TILLER GUARD - HEIGHT TO CLEAR MOTOR

2 H.P. MOTOR

TRANSVERSE BOTTOM FRAMES SIDED 1½"

PEAK HALYARD
THROAT HALYARD

FORESAIL SHEET

HORSE

STAYSAIL SHEET

FLOORBOARDS - REMOVABLE IN PORT & STARBOARD SECTIONS

JIB SHEET

HORSE

STAY'S'L SHEET P. & S.

FUEL TANK

MOTOR BOARD

WELL

THROAT HALYARD
PEAK HALYARD
MOORING CLEAT
JIB SHEET BULLSEYE
JIB TACK
JIB HALYARD

STAY'S'L TACK
STAY'S'L SHEET P. & S.

FORE & MAIN SHEETS BROUGHT AROUND MASTS TO CLEATS

SCALE 3/4" = 1'0"
DESIGN #345
23'6" x 5'0"
for Bob Wainright

PHILIP C. BOLGER
DESIGNER
GLOUCESTER, MASSACHUSETTS

MAIN SHEET

STAYSAIL HALYARD

1 2 3 4

DAGGER-
BOARD
TRUNK
1/4";
3/4 x 1 1/2"
FASTEN-
ING
CLEATS

6" HALYARD CLEATS
BOLTED THROUGH DECK

DAGGERBOARD
DOUBLE 1/2" TO
MAKE 1"; SEE
SHEET 3 FOR
PROFILE

MAST STEPS
DOUBLE 1/4" ON
1 1/2" SQ. FEET

FIT SHELVES
AS NEEDED

MIDSHIP SECTION

1'0"

SNAP HOOK ON SHEET
STANDING END

HORSE 1/2" NYLON

8"

SECTION 1'9" FOR'D OF TRANSOM

6 1/2° SIDE BEVEL

1' 5 3/4"

1' 11 1/8"

1' 6 7/8"

BULKHEAD #4
(WATERTIGHT)

BOTTOM
BEVEL 4°

1' 5 3/4"

BOWSPRIT
1 1/2" x 5 1/2"

1' 7 1/2"

9 3/4"

1' 2 1/2"

BULK-
HEAD
#1

9"

BOTTOM
BEVEL 3 1/2°

1' 7 1/2"

SIDE BEVEL 14°

SCALE 1 1/2" = 1'0"

DESIGN # 395
23'6" x 5'0"
for Bob Wainwright

PHILIP C. BOLGER
DESIGNER
GLOUCESTER, MASSACHUSETTS

12° SIDE BEVEL

1' 6 1/8"

1' 1 1/2"

TRANSOM

1' 2 3/4"

1' 5 1/2"

18°

SIDE BEVEL 3 1/2°

20°

6 1/2° SIDE BEVEL

2' 3 1/2"

1' 6 7/8"

1' 10 5/8"

BULKHEAD #2

BOTTOM BEVEL 1°

1' 7 1/2"

DIMENSIONS TO INSIDE OF
PLANK BEFORE BEVELLING.
ALL BEVELS ARE CONSTANT
PLYWOOD UNBEVELLED
SIDE IN EVERY BULKHEAD.

'REQUIRED READING: 'S. PAYSON
INSTANT BOATS' BY
INTERNATIONAL MARINE PUB. CO.

TRAIL KNEES 3/4"

4 1/4"

1 3/4"
11"
5 1/4"
4 5/8"
6"
5/8"
6"
10"
6"
11"
6"
11"
6"
11 1/4"

FALSE STEM
SIDED 3/4"

DECK @ SIDE
FULL SIZE

13°

CHINE
FULL SIZE

STEM
FULL SIZE

20°

13°

DECK STIFFENER
3/4" x 5 1/2" x 2.2"

2' 4 1/2"

1' 8"

1' 11 5/8"

BULKHEAD #3
NO BEVEL ON
ANY EDGE

1' 7 1/2"

SIDES & DECK 1/4" 1/4" = 1/2"
DOOR DOUBLE 1/4" = 1/2"
CLAMP & SHOE FROM 1 1/2" SQUARE
CHINE 3/4" x 1/2"
BULKHEADS & TRANSOM 1/4"
BACKING FRAMES 3/4", 2 1/2"; 3/4"; 1 1/2" IN WAY OF BULKHEADS
DECK STRINGERS 3/4", 2 1/2"

Scooner, Sheet 2.

Scooner, Sheet 3.

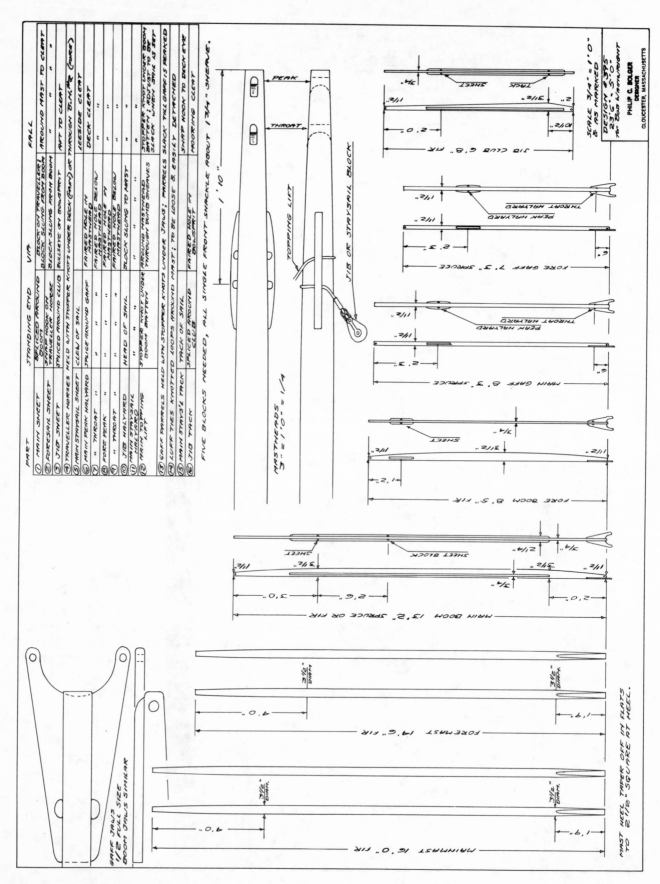

Scooner, Sheet 4.

Phil's four sheets of drawings are quite detailed, with critical items or areas keyed by number to a list of explanatory descriptions. Rather than give detailed step-by-step instructions, I'll cover the basics and high spots as I go along. You'll be able to fill in gaps from the discussions of the other Instant Boats in this book.

To build her hull sides, bulkheads, and decks, you need at least six sheets of plywood—seven, if you don't take scrupulous pains to utilize every possible square inch. Use ¼-inch 4-by-8-foot AC exterior plywood. You would need six more of the same to build the laminated double ¼-inch bottom specified. This lamination would make for a stronger bottom but is more work than I think is justified considering the minimal return—one which in my view is uncalled for. Instead, I would buy three sheets of ½-inch 4-by-8-foot AC exterior grade for the purpose.

By now, the following steps must have a familiar ring: Lay out the boat's sides on three sheets of plywood butted end to end; mark the locations of the frame molds on the sides, lay out the frame molds, cut, and tack to the sides in an upside-down assembly. Take note that before the final assembly, you must cut notches in the frame molds for the inside chine logs.

Chances are you will not find 2 x 4s long enough for the chine logs and gunwales of a craft of this length. I would use 16-footers and scarf them to the required length with a simple tapered glued joint, letting the joints in both the gunwales and the chine logs fall where they may on the hull.

I am not suggesting that you taper and glue these joints as you are installing the chine logs and gunwales. Make the tapers, assemble the joints, and glue them on your shop floor or on some level surface where they can set up undisturbed until you're ready to slip them into place.

There's one more step before you install the chine logs: Give them a constant 13-degree bevel. This permits an exact fit of the bottom to the chine logs, after you have taken down the high outboard edges of the side panels.

Once the sides are fastened to the bulkheads or frame molds and the chine logs are in place, the bottom goes on. Draw a fore-and-aft centerline on both faces of the three ½-inch plywood sheets. Tack the aftermost sheet to the transom temporarily, and match the centerline on the bottom to the centerlines on the transom and number 4 bulkhead. Slip a 6-inch butt strap right under the forward end of this bottom sheet, and fit its ends to the side panels. Do this right on the hull; it yields the most accurate fit. Fit the after-bottom panel to the sides, pie crust fashion, take it off, and saw it to shape. Replace it and fasten with glue and nails. Use the same procedure for constructing the rest of the bottom, making sure that all centerlines match up. The symmetry of the hull depends on this alignment, so don't slight it. With the forward-bottom panel on, the centerlines of the individual sections should line up as you sight along them, straight as looking down a gun barrel.

If you choose to construct a double bottom from ¼-inch ply, you should stagger the joints of the individual sheets by about 6 inches.

Now, using your overall centerline and working from outside the hull, bore holes for the fastenings of the bottom shoe; stagger the holes a little, laterally, to preserve strength. Apply glue, and drive fastenings from the inside while a helper holds a backing iron or heavy maul against the bottom to reduce bounce.

These are the essentials of building the hull, and when you have got her as far as this, you are in good shape to proceed on your own, following the plans.

I would like to point out that neither the daggerboard and its trunk nor the rudder pose as much of a challenge as they do in Gypsy.

Probably the most demanding step, in terms of skill, is the shaping of the schooner's masts. And yet, in practical terms, it is the least critical. It really doesn't matter if the masts are not perfectly round or if their tapers are less than perfect—except, perhaps, to the builder.

Even though I've made my share of spars, I'm no pro in this field. I am still bothered by the niceties of trying to produce a smooth taper while keeping the spars neatly rounded.

But first, let's see what we'll be working with. We'll begin with four 2 x 4s, 16 feet long, to make her two 3½-inch diameter masts. Two of them glued together will make the 16-foot mainmast, and the other two, the 14-foot 6-inch foremast.

You will get the best glue line by inspecting the growth lines of the sticks and putting the two concave faces together. This ensures that their edges will mate tightly. Place clamps about every foot, and support the glued pairs securely to prevent sagging while the glue is setting.

When you're ready to start shaping, lay one of your embryo masts across a couple of sawhorses, and scribe diagonals through the corners at the heel end to establish the center. Set your dividers at 1¾ inches to swing the 3½-inch diameter; this will show you how much you must take off the corners to bring the stick to round. But first establish the taper. The plan doesn't show the diameter of the truck, the top of the mast, but your scale rule will tell you it's to be 2 inches in diameter, so scribe a 2-inch circle around the center of that end.

Both the fore and main masts are tapered on the flat

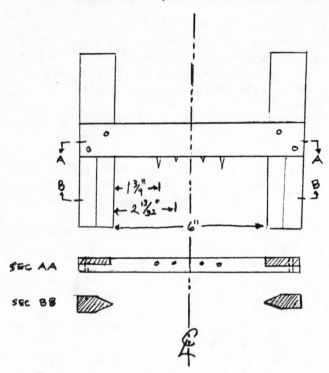

Gauge for marking spar stock for eight- and sixteen-siding.

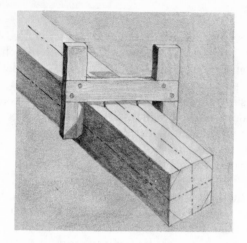

Marking spar stock for eight-siding.

to form a 2½-inch square at the heel, or lower end, where they are stepped. Above this, both are rounded to a 3½-inch diameter up to a point 4 feet below the truck, where they begin to taper to the 2-inch diameter of the truck itself.

I would draw and cut the taper, and then repeat on each freshly cut face. Now you have a tapered mast, still square in cross section.

The next step is to eight-side it, removing wood from the corners so that it becomes octagonal in cross section. Follow up by sixteen-siding it, which brings it close enough to round that you can finish it off with a small plane and some sandpaper.

In this eight-siding process, do not make the mistake of taking the same amount of wood off the corners the whole length of the mast right through the taper. If you do, you will end up with a slightly blunted over-sized pencil that is too small at the truck. I've done this job mostly by the eyeball method, but the end result of this by-guess-and-by-God approach has never really satisfied me. There is a device that greatly simplifies the process, which I just recently came across while looking through *Small Boat Building* by Dave Gannaway, published by Nautical Publishing Company, an English firm, in 1976. He casually mentions what he calls the spar gauge.

The accompanying drawing shows how you can make a spar gauge in a size suitable for the small spars we're concerned with. It has two sets of sharply pointed nails—a long outer pair and a shorter inner pair—and two angled, inward-facing cuts, one at each end. Push it along a square spar, and the long nails automatically scribe the lines for eight-siding. Repeat the process after you've eight-sided your spar, and the two shorter nails will scribe it for sixteen-siding. I've never seen nor heard of this spar gauge from any other source. Its great advantage is that it is self-adjusting to any square stick that's not too large, which means that you can ride it right through the taper, drawing the cut lines as you go.

The Light Schooner's fore and main gaffs are made of 1½-inch square spruce cut from slices of 2 x 4s; her booms are cut from ¾-inch-by-3½-inch spruce or fir boards, and their sides are stiffened by a piece of ¾-inch square stock; the club for her jib is the same.

A number of books devote some space to making the various types of spars—square, rectangular, and round, hollow and solid, with all the in-betweens, but I don't know of any one book exclusively devoted to the subject. I do know that whenever a master practitioner of the art, like the late Herbert Newbert of the Newbert and Wallace shipyard in Thomaston, was kind enough to discuss the fine points with me, I soon got lost in the explaining and dared not press my luck for further elaboration.

Even though you may not know a peak halyard from a topping lift, rigging this craft won't be difficult if you follow the plans. The numbers in the boxed section in the upper right-hand part of the spar plan sheet relate to the numbers on the sail plan drawing. By the time you've built and rigged her, you will know what all the parts are and what they are for.

APPENDIXES

APPENDIX I.
FEET, INCHES, EIGHTHS

All marine architects, in labeling dimensions on plans or compiling tables of offsets to establish shapes, follow the rule of feet, inches, and eighths of inches. Thus every such measurement is made up of three numbers. If you see 2-5-6, for example, the measurement in question is 2 feet, 5 inches, and ⅚ of an inch, and you can immediately convert the last figure to ¾. And 3-4-4 is 3 feet, 4½ inches. If there is a plus or a minus after the last figure, it means you add or subtract ⅟₁₆ inch.

Sometimes Phil Bolger departs from this practice to write in measurements such as 23½ inches, particularly when he has a series of such measurements in a small space, but his meaning is clear; he has simply gotten rid of what would be a cumbersome jumble of numerals. He does this on a number of his Instant Boat plans.

Just for practice, what is 10-9-7+? The answer is 10 feet 9 ¹⁵⁄₁₆ inches; the 7 represents ⅞ inch and the plus adds ⅟₁₆ inch.

I suggest that when you take measurements directly off a plan by means of your architect's scale rule, you write down your result in terms of feet, inches, and eighths, just to keep your hand in.

A note of caution here. Although an entire set of plans may be noted as drawn to a scale of 1½ inches equals 1 foot, when you're working with detail drawings or inserts, make sure that you're not overlooking a little label that says that this particular portion of the sheet is drawn to some other scale. When it is, it will be specified.

APPENDIX II.
AUDEL ON QUARTER SAWING LUMBER

I have taken the accompanying illustration and a portion of the text from my 1923 edition of *Audel's Carpenters and Builders Guide #1.*

The four methods of quarter sawing are shown in Fig. 8, each quadrant, a, b, c, d, of the log illustrating one of the methods.

The radial method, shown in quadrant a, is the best but gives the most waste. The cuts are taken along radii, or in the direction of the medullary rays. This method is the best not only on account of the handsomer surface but also because it will hold its shape better than when sawed by other methods. The reason for this is that the board shrinks most in a direction parallel with the annual rings, hence when radially sawed this shrinkage

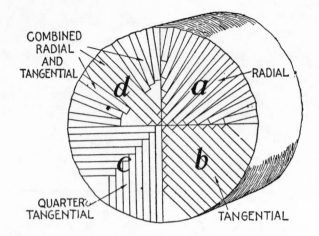

COMBINED RADIAL AND TANGENTIAL

d

a

RADIAL

QUARTER TANGENTIAL

c

b

TANGENTIAL

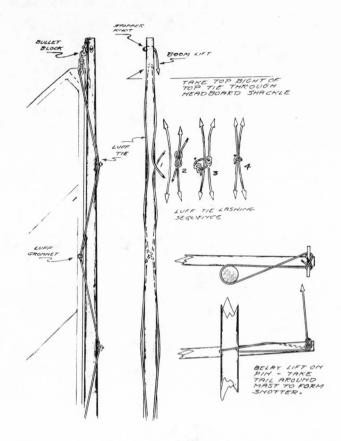

BULLET BLOCK

STOPPER KNOT

BOOM LIFT

TAKE TOP BIGHT OF TOP TIE THROUGH HEADBOARD SHACKLE

LUFF TIE

1   2   3   4

LUFF TIE LASHING SEQUENCE

LUFF GROMMET

BELAY LIFT ON PIN - TAKE TAIL AROUND MAST TO FORM SNOTTER.

is normal to the surface of the board and accordingly the warping is minimum.

Don't let that date of 1923 throw you. Of the four volumes Audel published, I consider myself lucky to have only the first. It covers a great deal of what any good carpenter should know or should learn. It is loaded with excellent information with clear illustrations and reflects the excellence of craftsmanship that Audel expected of every professional user of tools. He heads the page describing the contents with: "By hammer and hand all things do stand." And in his Foreword he says:

"When we build, let us think that we build forever. Let it not be for present delight nor for present use alone. Let it be such work as our descendants will thank us for; and let us think, as we lay stone on stone, that a time is to come when those stones will be held sacred because our hands have touched them, and that men will say, as they look upon the labor and wrought substance of them, 'See! This our father did for us.'"

To be sure, Audel is speaking of houses, not boats, but I like to think that those same high standards still apply. Houses or boats, when we talk of lumber we are talking about understanding the fundamental characteristics of wood and the tools we apply to it.

APPENDIX III.
MY FAVORITE LUFF-TIE SYSTEM

I admit that wooden masthoops are pretty, they go up and down with slippery ease, and you can even use

them as rungs to climb the mast if you've got a halyard stuck up there. You can't climb a sail track, but undoubtedly it produces the neatest possible fit of sail to mast, and it facilitates the unbending of the sail for bagging.

But Phil Bolger's luff tie beats them hollow for easy installation. It works perfectly for hoisting and dropping the sail, and it costs no more than the price of a few yards of line.

It's not called for in any of the boats presented in this book, but it doesn't hurt to expand your bag of tricks if you're going to be building boats on your own.

It first showed up in the plans for a 15-foot peapod Phil Bolger designed for me. It turned up again on Phil's very experimental Query (it has bow steering), and I had to come to grips with it to meet his delivery date. For ease of hoisting and dousing the sail, it delighted me.

To make it up:

Lay the mast across some supports, and with the luff stretched taut along it, lead your first line through the two uppermost cringles or reinforced grommets and tie the ends together midway between, making the ends long enough for another knot. You now have two lengths of line, one either side of the sail, running between the cringles. Bring those two lengths forward, one on each side of the mast, and tie them together with a second knot, using the long free ends of the first knot. At this point, there should be no slack. Repeat the process, working down to the foot, leading each successive line through the lower cringle of the previously completed tie and through the next cringle down.

It's simplicity itself. But it will permit your sail to be hoisted smartly and easily, it will keep a taut luff in a breeze, and it will come down in a rush when you let slip the halyard. If the tie is too tight or too slack, causing a bag in the sail's luff, just adjust the offending tie or ties until it's smooth all along its length.

Once you get the ties right, they stay that way. Query's did, all through a long winter of storage.

APPENDIX IV.
SCARFING PLYWOOD

When the construction of any of the Instant Boats requires the lengthening of a piece of plywood beyond the standard 8-foot dimension, its plans call for butting two pieces end-to-end or edge-to-edge, with a third piece overlapping them and acting as a butt strap. There is an alternative method used by plywood manufacturers to make larger sheets. It is called scarfing; in it the meeting ends are tapered, and the tapered areas are overlapped and secured by glue without benefit of a butt strap. This means that the thickness of the jointure remains the same as the thickness of the individual members. As executed by the plywood manufacturers, scarfing makes a very neat and smooth joint.

I'll describe the process here for the use of any Instant Boat builder who wishes to undertake it; I have always used the butt-strap approach in building these craft. The only time I went in for scarfing was the result of a windfall in plywood of a very unusual length. Nothing starts you thinking like having a pile of nice marine plywood on hand, all of which is 2 feet too short to suit your purposes.

These sheets were $5/16$ inch by 4 feet by 14 feet, unusual both in thickness and in length. The owner of the local boat shop where I bought it must have been wondering what to do with it, too, as it had been lying around there for years with only a few sheets of it used. Eventually I asked the owner for a price on the whole

pile of some 30 sheets, and he gave me one I couldn't resist. I figured that even if I couldn't scarf it out a couple of feet for the boats I had in mind to build, I could still use every scrap of my Triple A Grade Royal Marine plywood one way or another, in view of its bargain price compared with then-current levels.

So I stuck it in a corner of my shop and began poring over every book or article I could find that might show me a good, clear picture of a ready-made scarf joint and clear instructions on how to do it. All I turned up was the basic procedure and a scale ratio of width of the joint to plywood thickness. Just about all my sources gave a ratio of 12 to 1, which was at least a start.

Working from the 12 to 1 ratio, I shaded it a trifle and drew my scarf boundaries $3\frac{1}{2}$ inches from the ends of the two pieces I was going to join. I wanted these joints to be right, because they would form the aft ends of the sides of the Gloucester Light Dories I was building, and the joints were free standing—nailed only at the gunwale and the chine log. So I did some practicing on odd scraps first, beginning with a series of cuts with my Skilsaw set on a fixed inclined plane, which didn't work.

Next I tried a sharp hand plane, which, by the way, was the tool most often recommended in the articles I'd read. But that tore up the cross-grain and was terribly slow besides. It gave me a very strong desire to watch someone else do it with a hand plane. I was beginning to feel that the whole pile could just go on sitting there, for all the luck I was having.

So I adopted a what-have-I-got-to-lose attitude; I grabbed my electric hand plane and went at it eyeball fashion.

I wanted to taper the joints to a feather edge because that's the only way they would go together without slipping endways. Doing this without destroying the wood was obviously a problem, so I supported the edge I was tapering on a flat piece of ½-inch aluminum (wood is just as good) and weighted the plywood down to keep the plane from chattering. My electric plane made short work of tapering a joint two feet long. Watching the veneers for straightness of cut, I stopped when I had mowed the taper down to within $1/16$ inch of a feather edge—as far as I thought I could go without splintering the very fragile taper—and finished it to a knife edge with a belt sander fitted with 60 grit paper.

I proved the joints for fairness with a straightedge, cemented them together with resorcinol glue in a sandwich of waxed paper over and under the joint along with boards clamped on both sides, and left them overnight for the scarf joint to cure. These sample joints not only looked good, they *were* good, as my over-the-knee tests demonstrated. When I splintered them this way, it was the wood that parted, not the glued joints.

I had never had the courage to tackle joints like this before, but now I would never hesitate to tackle them again. Once more I had convinced myself that dreading a job is far worse than doing it. I know that this is true, but it's the kind of thing you need to prove to yourself every once in a while. True, too, is the fact that often the solution to a tough job comes along only after you've started in on it.

If you do choose to scarf your joints instead of buttstrapping them, this process will shorten the length of the final product by the width of the scarf. Bear this in mind, and don't let yourself get caught short.

APPENDIX V.
LEARNING TO SAIL

One thing that sticks in my craw is the fact that all too many books and articles on sailing are slanted toward making it a mystery that no amateur can really hope to master. Too often the intention seems to be to impress the reader, and the fancy language in such "introductions" fosters the solemn-rite approach.

In actual fact, the basics of sailing are really quite simple. What you need is a strong dose of common sense and the development of a feel for the balance between sheet and tiller. If you feel you're being overpowered, ease your sheet or turn your rudder to make your boat head up into the wind. If she feels loggy, haul in on your sheet or drop off the wind a little more. Pretty quickly, these become automatic reactions and not the deliberate working out of any elaborate equation. You learned to ride a bicycle, didn't you?

Let's assume your Gypsy is tied up alongside a float, with a moderate breeze coming from dead ahead or angled slightly over the bow. You won't need such nearly ideal conditions in the future, but for now let's keep it easy. Oars and life jacket are ready to hand; you've hung the rudder, shoved the daggerboard home in its case or trunk, and stepped the mast. Now attach the after end of the sprit to the sheet, with the slot between the clew of the sail and the stopper knot on the sheet. The sheet is loosely but neatly coiled or flaked, and the sprit and the sail are loose, letting the wind push them where it will.

Next, shove the sprit aft to extend the sail. Engage its forward end with the snotter, cleating the snotter against the mast.

Cast off your dock lines and shove off with the sheet in one hand and the tiller in the other. Push the bow off hard enough to force it through the eye of the wind, so the wind will come to bear on the side of the bow toward the dock. This keeps the bow swinging away from the dock. Put your tiller "down"—toward the lee—and haul in on the sheet so the wind fills your sail. When you start to make headway, quickly put your tiller amidships to keep her just off the wind. You don't want to point directly into the wind and "get into irons"—that is, become stalled, with the wind blowing the sail straight back over the rudder and driving her backward. You are clear of the float and sailing.

Study the accompanying diagrams. Note the several points of sail. *Close hauled*, you point as close to the direction the wind is coming from as you can without luffing (heading up too close, causing the luff or leading edge of your sail to shake). In practice, this is about 45 degrees; if your boat can sail a smaller angle than that, consider it pure gravy. When the wind is coming from starboard and your sail is swung out to port, you are on a starboard tack; conversely, if the wind is coming from port, you are on a port tack.

On a *broad reach*, the wind comes from abaft the beam. Ease off on your sheet until you find the angle at which you get the most speed. If the wind is dead astern or nearly so—well abaft the beam, at any rate—you are *running free* before the wind. If the wind strikes the starboard quarter, you are running before the wind on the starboard tack, and conversely if it comes from over your port quarter. A variation, and a somewhat dangerous one, is when you are running before a quartering wind with the sail out on the same side that the wind is coming from: You are then sailing *by the lee* and in danger of jibing (more on that in a moment).

Obviously you can't sail directly into the wind, but you can *tack* your way toward that direction—sailing close hauled on one tack and *coming about* (turning) to sail close hauled on the other—making a series of tacks, first to one side and then to the other of the course you want to achieve or "make good."

If you have a passenger aboard, sing out your intentions so he or she can keep clear of the sail as it swings across the cockpit, and can shift over to the high, or weather, side at the same instant you do, to keep the boat as nearly upright as possible. (Heeling way over looks like speed, but it's not. Extreme heel reduces the effective sail area presented to the wind, and it generates a very inefficient underwater hull shape. Keep her upright if you can.)

I suggest you call out your warnings even when you're soloing, for a while, at least. When you are about to put your tiller down—toward the sail—sing out "Ready about!" When you shove the tiller over, give out

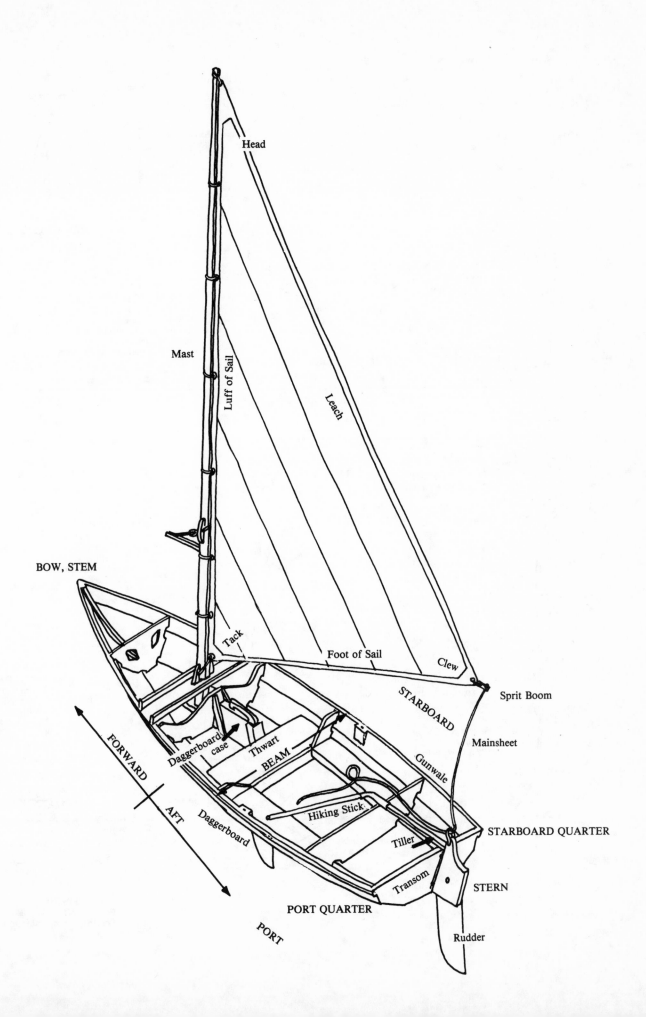

Head

Mast

Luff of Sail

Leach

BOW, STEM

Tack

Foot of Sail

Clew

STARBOARD

Sprit Boom

Mainsheet

Daggerboard case

Thwart

BEAM

Gunwale

FORWARD

Daggerboard

Hiking Stick

STARBOARD QUARTER

AFT

Tiller

PORT

Transom

STERN

PORT QUARTER

Rudder

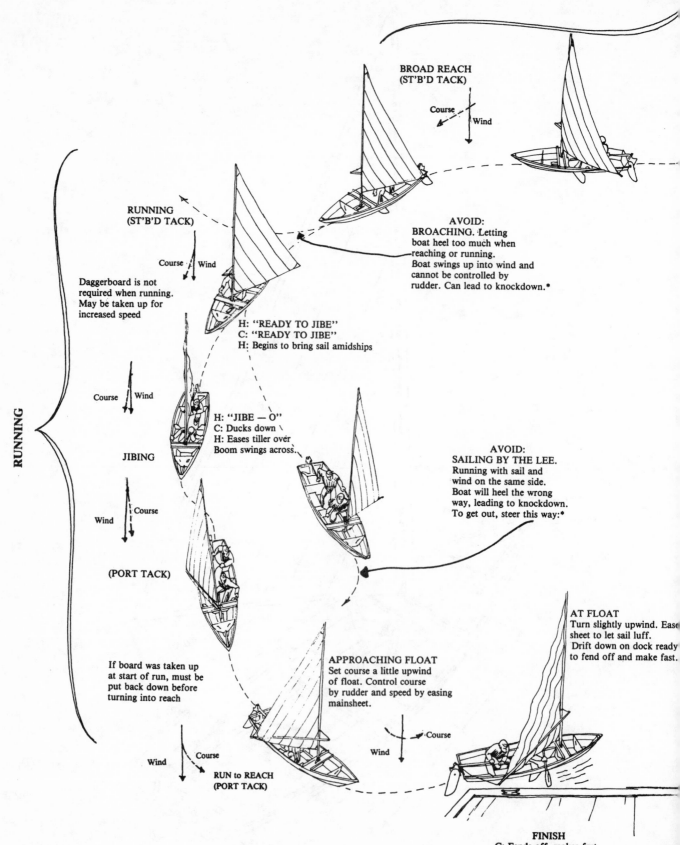

**BROAD REACH
(ST'B'D TACK)**

Course · Wind

**AVOID:
BROACHING.** Letting
boat heel too much when
reaching or running.
Boat swings up into wind and
cannot be controlled by
rudder. Can lead to knockdown.*

**RUNNING
(ST'B'D TACK)**

Course · Wind

Daggerboard is not
required when running.
May be taken up for
increased speed

H: "READY TO JIBE"
C: "READY TO JIBE"
H: Begins to bring sail amidships

Course · Wind

RUNNING

H: "JIBE — O"
C: Ducks down
H: Eases tiller over
Boom swings across.

JIBING

Wind · Course

**AVOID:
SAILING BY THE LEE.**
Running with sail and
wind on the same side.
Boat will heel the wrong
way, leading to knockdown.
To get out, steer this way:*

(PORT TACK)

AT FLOAT
Turn slightly upwind. Ease
sheet to let sail luff.
Drift down on dock ready
to fend off and make fast.

If board was taken up
at start of run, must be
put back down before
turning into reach

APPROACHING FLOAT
Set course a little upwind
of float. Control course
by rudder and speed by easing
mainsheet.

Wind · Course

Wind · Course

**RUN to REACH
(PORT TACK)**

FINISH
C: Fends off, makes fast.
Boat rig, board, and rudder
unshipped.

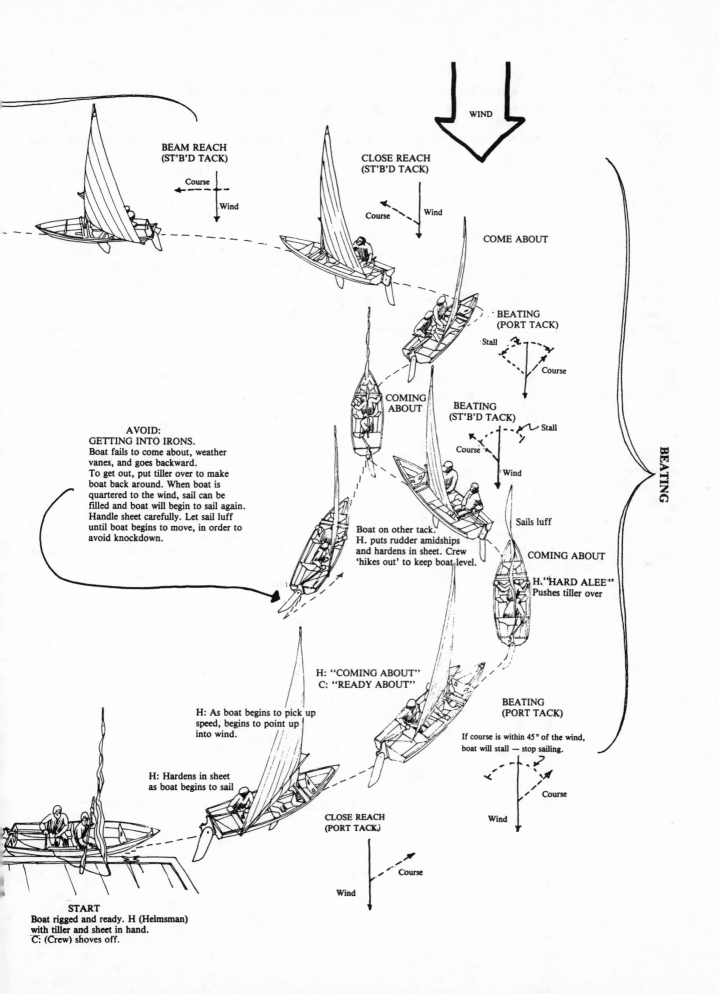

BEAM REACH
(ST'B'D TACK)

Course ←
Wind ↓

CLOSE REACH
(ST'B'D TACK)

Course ←
Wind ↓

WIND

COME ABOUT

BEATING
(PORT TACK)

Stall
Course

COMING
ABOUT

BEATING
(ST'B'D TACK)

Course ←
Stall
Wind ↓

AVOID:
GETTING INTO IRONS.
Boat fails to come about, weather
vanes, and goes backward.
To get out, put tiller over to make
boat back around. When boat is
quartered to the wind, sail can be
filled and boat will begin to sail again.
Handle sheet carefully. Let sail luff
until boat begins to move, in order to
avoid knockdown.

Boat on other tack.
H. puts rudder amidships
and hardens in sheet. Crew
'hikes out' to keep boat level.

Sails luff

COMING ABOUT

H. "HARD ALEE"
Pushes tiller over

BEATING

H: "COMING ABOUT"
C: "READY ABOUT"

H: As boat begins to pick up
speed, begins to point up
into wind.

BEATING
(PORT TACK)

If course is within 45° of the wind,
boat will stall — stop sailing.

Course

Wind ↓

H: Hardens in sheet
as boat begins to sail

CLOSE REACH
(PORT TACK)

Course

Wind ↓

START
Boat rigged and ready. H (Helmsman)
with tiller and sheet in hand.
C: (Crew) shoves off.

with a firm "Hard alee!" As soon as the bow has turned through the wind (actually a little earlier, when you've got the hang of it) gently ease off your tiller position to catch her before she swings too far into the other tack.

Tacking, you are always turning through the wind. When you change your heading by *jibing*, you turn away from the wind and let it cross over behind the after edge, or leech, of the sail. This is safely done only under rigid control. In a controlled jibe, you tend the sheet continuously, always keeping tension on it, so the sail doesn't slam over. You should have the sail trimmed flat when the wind crosses the leech, then ease it out on your new point of sail. Uncontrolled or accidental jibes snap off masts, knock people overboard, and wreak general havoc. So practice your jibes in very light winds, for a start.

There is one situation in which a controlled, intentional jibe is well worth it. If someone has fallen overboard, or you lose a piece of gear over the side and want to retrieve it, a correctly executed jibe allows you to pass right over the very water in which the accident occurred, but you can tack all day and never get within an arm's reach of what you're trying to recover. Sail on a short way before you jibe, the necessary distance depending on the turning radius of the boat.

It can also be a useful maneuver, *sometimes*, to avoid some hazard in the water or to reduce the number of tacks you must make to reach your destination. But don't get too casual about it. Practice it enough so that you're not mortally afraid of it, and you can execute a jibe when it really is called for.

Now for the commandment that gets dinned into the ears of every sailor—one that every sailor sometimes disregards. DON'T MAKE FAST YOUR SHEET. Everyone is tempted, now and again, to cleat the sheet or actually tie it. Don't.

Oh, OK—under mill pond conditions, go ahead. But even then, I recommend only two or three turns around a cleat and no locking half hitch to hold it down, so you can throw it off in an instant.

Just as important, keep your sheet neatly coiled or loosely flaked, so it won't get tangled or demonstrate its uncanny ability to tie knots in itself. It has got to be free to run. With an unstayed rig like Gypsy's, you can avoid a knockdown from the most sudden and violent gust just by letting the sheet go, allowing the wind to blow the sail out in any direction it may choose—as long as it's not snarled up, caught on some projection, or tied. You can regain control of it when things calm down. Until they do, let it blow, let it go.

Under really catastrophic conditions, you can unstep your mast and throw the whole rig overboard. Towed astern by the sheet, it will function as a sea anchor and keep your stern facing the wind. You can use your oars to maneuver around and gather it all in when things calm down.

Sail your Instant Boat in protected waters. That needn't restrict you to landlocked basins, but it does put a no-no on allowing yourself to succumb to the lure of the open sea.

Have fun.

Glossary

Abaft. Aft of, as in, "A schooner's mainmast is abaft the foremast."

Aft. Toward the stern.

After. Closer to the stern.

Amidships. In the middle portion of a boat. As an adjective, "midships."

Athwartships. Running across the hull. As an adjective, "thwartship."

Baseline. A line, usually parallel to the waterline, drawn on boat plans and used as a reference for all vertical measurements when lofting the lines of a hull.

Batten. A thin, flat length of wood that can be sprung through a series of reference points and thereby used to determine and draw a fair curve through the points.

Bevel. An angle cut along the edge of a timber or across its end to produce an exact fit between parts of a hull.

Bilge. The lower internal region of a hull, or (often as "turn of the bilge") the region of maximum curvature between the bottom and sides in a cross-sectional view of a round-bottomed boat.

Breasthook. A thwartship structural member near the stem.

Bulkhead. A thwartship panel dividing a hull into sections. Equivalent to a frame mold in an Instant Boat.

Butt. To join end-to-end or edge-to-edge. As a noun, a butt strap or butt block fastened across such a joint to hold the two elements together. Also, the lower end of a mast.

Carvel Planking. A method of planking in which the strakes or planks are fastened to the frames of a hull edge to edge.

Centerboard. A short, hinged, retractable keel used to reduce leeway in a sailboat. It is raised and lowered through a watertight case, or trunk.

Centerline. On boat plans, a line dividing a hull into two identical fore-and-aft sections, and used as a base for establishing thwartship measurements when lofting. Also, a vertical line on thwartship members used to align them during assembly.

Chine. A longitudinal joint where panel edges meet in a hull constructed of a sheet material such as plywood. Most commonly, the joint between sides and bottom in a flat- or V-bottomed boat.

Chine Log. A reinforcing strip of wood along the inside or outside of a chine, to which the joining panels are fastened.

Cleat. A fitting to which a line can be made fast. A protruding wooden or metal fitting on a spar, functioning to limit the movement of the spar through an aperture, such as a cleat on a mast that stops its downward movement through a mast partner. Finally, any short length of small dimensional lumber used for miscellaneous framing needs.

Clew. The lower, aftermost corner of a sail.

Close-hauled. One of the points of sailing, said of a sailboat that is pointing up into the wind as far as it can without luffing.

Cringle. A reinforced aperture in a sail, such as a metal grommet, through which a line can be passed.

Daggerboard. A type of centerboard that, instead of being hinged, is raised or lowered in its case vertically by means of lifting handles.

Deadrise. The upward slant of the bottom of a hull to the chine in a V-bottomed hull, or from the keel to the turn of the bilge in a round-bottomed hull.

Dory. A flat-bottomed craft that has flaring sides and a narrow stern. It is capable of carrying heavy loads but is very tender when light.

Double-ended. Having a sharp end at both bow and stern (e.g., a canoe or a peapod).

Edge-nailed. A method of planking in which successive narrow strakes, usually square or nearly so, are fastened together with nails and generally glued as well.

Edge-set. In a carvel-planked boat, to drive one plank down forcibly to meet the plank below despite irregularities in the planks.

Face. The flat, broad surface of a board or timber.

Fair. Said of a graceful curve that changes gradually and has no bumps, hollows, or flat places. Used also as a verb.

Flare. The outward angle of a boat's sides between waterline and sheer when viewed in cross section.

Flitch. A plank or board that has the natural shape of a tree and still has its bark.

Flush. Even or level with, not protruding.

Foot. The bottom edge of a sail. Also, the butt of a mast.

Frame or Frame Mold. A thwartship member to which planking is fastened.

Framing Piece. A strengthening member fastened to the edge of a bulkhead or transom to add rigidity.

Freeboard. At any given point along a hull, the height of the sheer above the waterline.

Gaff. The spar to which the head of a gaff sail is lashed. It has a set of jaws that run up or down the mast when the sail is hoisted or lowered.

Gaff-headed. Describing a sailing rig such as the Light Schooner has, consisting of quadrilateral fore-and-aft sails fitted with gaffs.

Garboard. In a carvel-planked boat, the plank next to the keel, either port or starboard.

Grommet. A round, metal eyelet or a ring of rope sewn into a sail or other piece of cloth.

Gudgeon. A metal eye or other aperture installed on the keel, skeg, or transom of a boat, into which the rudder pintles fit when the rudder is shipped or installed.

Gunwale. The longitudinal strengthening strip that runs along the sheer of a hull from bow to stern. (Pronounced gunn'l)

Gusset. A stiffening bracket fastened to any two structural members where they meet at an angle near 90 degrees.

Halyard. The line, reeved through a block or similar device, with which the sail is raised.

Head. The top corner of a jibheaded sail or the top edge of a quadrilateral sail. In a gaff rig, the head of the sail is attached to the gaff; in a lug rig it is attached to the upper yard.

Heel. As a verb, the tendency of a sailboat to lean from the vertical in response to the pressure of the wind on the sails. Also used as a noun in that sense, as in "the angle of heel." Also as a noun, the foot or butt of the mast or the end of a frame at the keel (in a carvel-planked hull).

Horse. A transverse metal rod, metal loop, or loop of line that the inboard portion of a sheet can travel along, allowing the boom or the jib club to swing across the hull without being tended when making short tacks: traveler.

Inboard. Within the limits of the hull area.

Jaws. A U-shaped fitting on the inboard end of a boom or gaff that allows the spar to swing around the mast.

Jib. A triangular sail set forward of the mast.

Jibe. To change course by turning away from the wind and letting it pass around the leech of the sail.

Jibheaded. Describes a triangular sail, without a gaff.

Jig. A wooden structure on a fixed base on which the parts of a boat can be assembled. A jig determines the shape of the part.

Keel. The main structural member and longitudinal backbone of a hull; it usually extends below the hull to help keep the boat on a heading and reduce leeway.

Knee. A strengthening timber that is fastened to two angled members and distributes stress to both.

Knot. A measure of speed equal to 1 nautical mile (2,000 yards) per hour. It is incorrect to say "knots per hour."

Lapstrake. A method of planking in which each strake slightly overlaps the one below it, giving the appearance of clapboards.

Lee. Away from the direction of the wind. A lee shore is leeward (pronounced loo-ard) of the viewer's boat, and is a good place to stay away from in a blow.

Leeboard. A board mounted outboard on a boat that serves the same purpose as a centerboard or daggerboard but can be moved to port or starboard in order always to be on the leeward side.

Leech. The after edge of a fore-and-aft sail.

Leeway. Motion through the water of a boat being driven sideways by the wind (sometimes applied to motion induced by current or tide).

Limber Holes. Apertures in bulkheads that allow water in the bilge to move from one section of the hull to another.

Lofting. The process of laying out the patterns of the parts of a hull full size, working from plans drawn to scale.

Loose-footed. Having no boom or other spar along the foot of the sail.

Luff. As a verb, to head up into the wind so much that the forward edge of the sail begins to shake. As a noun, the forward edge of a fore-and-aft sail.

Lugsail. A quadrilateral sail that is rigged with yards at its head and foot, and set against a mast so that a portion of its area extends forward of the mast. Windsprint carries a "standing lug," in which the yards are always on the same side of the mast. A "dipping lug" has a boom on the foot with jaws set against the mast; it is lowered when changing tacks, and the upper yard is moved to the other side of the mast. A boat rigged with several lugsails is called a "lugger."

Mast. The vertical spar that is the main support column of the sailing rig.

Mast Partner. A transverse member located at a height just below the sheerline of a boat, through which the mast passes to acquire steadiness and bearing.

Mast Rings. Rings attached to the luff of a sail that are used in hoisting and lowering the sail and that keep the luff taut. Traditionally made of wood, mast rings are sometimes made of metal or plastic.

Maul. A hammer similar to a small sledge, weighing as much as 4 pounds.

Mold. A pattern of a transverse section of a hull, set up in construction but removed when the hull nears completion. A frame mold acts as a mold but remains in the finished hull.

Mooring. A method of anchoring in which a boat is made fast to a heavy weight that is more or less permanently fixed to the bottom.

Nail Set. A steel rod that has a small, blunt end and is used to drive a nailhead flush with the wood or to countersink it slightly below the surface. It is placed on the nailhead and struck with a hammer.

Offsets. A table of measurements from the baseline and centerline that establish points defining the shape of a hull. Offsets are used to loft and lay down the lines of a boat full size.

Outboard. Outside the limits of the hull, or in a direction away from the centerline.

Painter. A line made fast to the bow of a boat and used for temporary tie-ups and for towing.

Peak. In a gaff sail, the after upper corner of the quadrilateral.

Pintle. A vertical pin or rod used to hang or hinge a rudder. Pintles are attached to the forward or leading edge of the rudder and slide into gudgeons fixed to the stern of a boat. (See *Gudgeon.*)

Prebore. To bore a hole in wood that a nail or other fastening will be driven into. Preboring reduces the danger of breaking out or splitting. The holes should be slightly smaller than the wire diameter of the shank of the fastening.

Quarter. One of the two outboard quadrants of a boat's stern. May also be used as a verb: A boat is said to be *quartering into the seas* when its bow is directed slightly to port or starboard of a steep head sea.

Rabbet. A beveled recess cut into the stem to receive the forward, or hood, ends of the planking and into the keel to receive the lower edge of the garboard strake.

Rake. A departure from the vertical of any member of a boat, such as the stem, transom, or mast.

Reach. A point of sailing. A boat is on a broad reach when the wind is coming from abaft the beam, and on a close reach when the wind is coming from forward of the beam but abaft the close-hauled position.

Run. The curve of the bottom of a hull as it rises from a point near amidships toward the stern. If the rise is gentle, with little rocker, the boat is said to have a flat run.

Running Free. Describes a boat that is sailing before the wind, or nearly so. The wind is coming over the stern of the boat.

Scarf. As a verb, to glue two beveled pieces of wood end to end or edge to edge; beveling allows the pieces to overlap without an increase in thickness. As a noun, describes a joint so made.

Schooner. A fore-and-aft rigged craft that has two masts, the mainmast, or aftermast, being the taller. Larger schooners have been rigged with as many as seven masts.

Scuppers. Holes or open pipes above a boat's waterline that drain water overboard.

Seam. The joint between two planks or strakes, rendered watertight by caulking.

Seize. To bind together; or, to put a stopper on a line. Line for seizing is always smaller and lighter than the line to which it is applied.

Sheer. The uppermost line of a hull viewed in profile, also called the sheerline. The top plank, or strake, on a hull is the sheerstrake.

Sheet. A line used to control the positioning of a sail in relation to the wind. On a sail attached to a boom, the sheet is made fast to the boom near its outboard end; on a loose-footed sail, it is attached to the clew.

Shim. To wedge up or fill out with thin sheets of metal or wood.

Shutter. The strake that closes in a hull that has been planked both up from the keel and down from the sheer; the bilge panel in a Tack-and-Tape hull.

Sloop. A fore-and-aft rigged sailboat that has one mast and carries a jib.

Snotter. A line that bears on or near the butt of a sprit to maintain its thrust against either the clew of a jibheaded sail or the peak of a quadrilateral sail.

Spanish Windlass. A length of line looped around the planks or side panels of a hull to pull them into place, usually by means of a lever that twists the line and constricts the loop. In action it resembles a tourniquet.

Spar. Any timber (mast, boom, gaff, or sprit) used to support a sailing rig.

Spile. To determine and scribe a line that defines the shape of any element in a hull so that it will exactly fit an adjoining element as required. Most frequently, to transfer the shape of the upper edge of a plank or strake onto the bottom edge of the plank to be fastened immediately above it.

Sprit. A spar used to set a spritsail by extending the clew of a triangular sail or the peak of a quadrilateral sail.

Spritsail. Any sail set by means of a sprit.

Stem. The foremost vertical or nearly vertical structural member of a boat's hull; sometimes called a cutwater.

Step. As a verb, to erect and secure a mast in place on a boat. As a noun, any construction or device in the bottom of a hull that the butt end of a mast is set into.

Strake. A single unit of the planking that closes in a boat's hull.

Tack. As a verb, to change course by turning into and through the eye of the wind until its pressure falls on the other side of the sail. As a noun, the forward lower corner of any fore-and-aft sail.

Template. A pattern cut from wood, metal, or paper and used to scribe lines on building stock.

Tender. As a noun, a small boat used for general service to a larger boat. As an adjective, said of a boat that is quick to heel because of a shift in the load or pressure from the wind.

Throat. The forward upper corner of a quadrilateral fore-and-aft sail.

Thwart. A transverse member, often a seat for crew or passengers.

Topping Lift. In a fore-and-aft rig, a line reeved through a mast block to the end of the boom, used to support the weight of the boom to keep it clear of the cockpit or to facilitate lowering sail. The Light Schooner has topping lifts.

Transom. The after face of the stern of a boat; often, the entire stern.

Trim. As a noun, the fore-and-aft positioning of a hull in the water. As a verb, to alter that positioning, as in "trim her down by the bow." Also, to haul in on a sheet, bringing the clew of a fore-and-aft sail nearer the boat's centerline.

Truck. The very top of a mast, often called the masthead.

Trunk. A narrow boxlike structure, open to the sea at the bottom of the boat, through which a centerboard or daggerboard can be lowered to extend below the bottom; also called a case.

Tumblehome. The inward curve of the upper sides of a hull toward the centerline.

V-bottomed Boat. A chine boat whose deadrise is flat between the keel and the chine; sometimes called a deadrise boat.

Waterline. Any horizontal line on a boat's profile generated by a plane parallel to the surface of the water. The LWL, load waterline, is the upper limit of a boat's draft under normal conditions with the designed load.

Weather. Windward or toward the wind; opposite of leeward.

Weatherly. Said of a boat that is capable of performing safely and making progress to weather in adverse conditions of wind and sea.

Yard. A spar hung transversely across a mast to support and extend a quadrilateral sail. Windsprint's lug sail is spread between upper and lower yards.

Index